The All-American Girls After the AAGPBL

How Playing Pro Ball Shaped Their Lives

KAT D. WILLIAMS

McFarland & Company, Inc., Publishers

Jefferson, North Carolina

LIBRARY OF CONGRESS CATALOGUING-IN-PUBLICATION DATA

Names: Williams, Kat D., author.
Title: The all-American girls after the AAGPBL : how playing pro
   ball shaped their lives / Kat D. Williams.
Description: Jefferson, N.C. : McFarland & Company, Inc., 2017. |
   Includes bibliographical references and index.
Identifiers: LCCN 2017004534 | ISBN 9780786472352 (softcover :
   acid free paper) ∞
Subjects: LCSH: All-American Girls Professional Baseball League. |
   Women baseball players—United States—History. | Sports for
   women—United States—History.
Classification: LCC GV875.A56 W55 2017 | DDC 796.357/64—dc23
LC record available at https://lccn.loc.gov/2017004534

BRITISH LIBRARY CATALOGUING DATA ARE AVAILABLE

ISBN (print) 978-0-7864-7235-2
ISBN (ebook) 978-1-4766-2695-6

On the cover Maybelle Blair at the 2015 Baseball for All National
Tournament in Orlando, Florida (author collection)

Printed in the United States of America

*McFarland & Company, Inc., Publishers
   Box 611, Jefferson, North Carolina 28640
      www.mcfarlandpub.com*

For Greta Rensenbrink,
without whom this book would not exist.
With you, all things are possible.

Table of Contents

Acknowledgments

From its inception, this project benefited from the help and support of countless people, especially my mom and dad, TJ and Sara Williams. They taught me to love baseball and to appreciate and respect the significance of the game. It was my early connection to the game that saved me as a child and motivated me as an adult. To my sister and lifelong champion, Kim Williams, who made me laugh when humor was the only way forward and endured countless baseball events on my behalf, thank you. To my brother-in-law, Michael Hammond, whose zest for life inspired me and provided the extra motivation needed to finish this book, hoist!

To my Rensenbrink family, who provided summer retreats and unconditional love, support, and lobster, thank you. You will never know how much easier this task has been having the Rensenbrink force on my side.

To the dogs in my life—Little, Sea and Zelda Rose—I literally could not have done this without you.

One very important lesson I learned during the time spent on this book is that families are often made, not inherited. By 2005, I had met Maybelle Blair, Terry Donahue, Pat Henschel, Jane Moffet, Isabel Alvarez, Shirley Burkovich, and Kristen Huff. My life has been richer, happier, and more fulfilled because of them. Each and every one contributed to this book in innumerable ways. They are, and will forever be, family.

My extended baseball family, the team that makes up the International Women's Baseball Center—Perry Barber, Donna Cohen, Cami Kidder, and Debbie Pierson—never wavers in its support of women's baseball, and especially my role in it. Thank you for the example you set.

Acknowledgments

The faculty and staff of Marshall University's history department supported me and remained steadfast in their belief that I could write this book. From my first days at Marshall, Montserrat Miller took me under her wing and, through her own example, helped me believe, too. A special thanks to my colleagues, Bob Deal, Dan Holbrook, Donna Spindel, and Chris White, for their friendship, understanding, and encouragement.

Over the years I have had a number of bright, talented students. One such student, Kaitlyn Haines, worked as a research assistant on this book. Thank you.

A number of the research trips conducted on behalf of this project were made possible through the support of Marshall University's Quinlan and Inco programs. The project was also supported by two sabbaticals from Marshall University and its College of Liberal Arts.

Tim Wiles, director of research at the National Baseball Hall of Fame in 2002, first introduced me to the women of the All-American Girls Professional Baseball League (AAGPBL) and set this whole project in motion. Thank you.

To the women of the All-American Girls Professional Baseball League, thank you. Your strength and courage inspire me every day. It is my hope that this book does justice to your story and the lives you created after the league.

Preface

This book explores the role of sports in creating identity—in particular, the ways in which access to baseball affected the lives of the women who played in the All-American Girls Professional Baseball League (AAGPBL).

I began this project after a group of students challenged me to show them real-life examples of why and how sports were important to women. The AAGPBL players provide the lens through which I explore the themes of financial benefit, travel, exposure to diversity, patriotism, and, finally, the women's legacy.

Their salaries, high for women of the time, gave every player an opportunity to make more money than they might have obtained in what were then socially acceptable (and usually lower-paying) jobs. The fact that these women earned that money by playing professional baseball made the experience even better. Travel and the chance to encounter new people were important byproducts of life in the league. Many of the players were from small towns, and the opportunity to see and experience different places and cultures was invaluable, changing their lives more profoundly than any other benefit of playing in the league. Additionally, for some of the players and league personnel, patriotism and military service were connected to their time in the AAGPBL. Players' self-described "place in American history" and their role in what some have called a revolution in women's sports is still another focus of this book. In this narrative, the players' experiences and stories come together to paint a picture of the league's impact on these women.

Introduction

"A woman may take part in the grandstand, with applause for the brilliant play, with a waving kerchief to the hero.... But neither our wives, our sisters, our daughters, nor our sweethearts, may play Base Ball on the field.... Base Ball is too strenuous for wom-ankind."
                                   —Dorothy Seymour Mills and Harold Seymour[1]

As a woman who played softball in the years before the passage of Title IX (which requires schools receiving federal money to provide girls with equal opportunities in all areas, including sports), I am very protective of the legislation and sensitive to any measures that would weaken it. A few years ago, when I read about yet another attempt to strip Title IX of its power, I took the opportunity to discuss the issue in my women's history class. I asked my students whether they thought Title IX was still relevant. Some of the young women, many of them athletes, argued that women's sports are so much a part of modern society that women don't need this kind of "protection" anymore. It is easy to find examples of players who earn a good living and have made names for themselves in the world of sports, they said. These students pointed to golf star Michelle Wie and tennis greats like the Williams sisters to prove that female athletes have gained full access to the professional opportunities men have enjoyed for years. But others among my largely working-class students were not impressed by these examples. In their minds, those sports exude privilege, and the women who play them have lives my students could not relate to. "Poor people like us don't belong to the country club," they countered. Someone pointed out that we now have professional women's basketball with the WNBA (Women's National Basketball Association). Basketball is played in the streets and schoolyards, not in a country club. That's only one sport, I responded, and the WNBA is struggling to reach fans.

Another group of students—the non-sports-minded members of the class—were more dismissive. They argued that we have other, more important things to worry about, like equal opportunity in employment, housing, and education. "It's only sports," they said. I protested, explaining that equality is important regardless of the aspect of life in question. Sports can also provide very tangible advantages, such as a good salary and professional opportunities. Plus, I argued, sports give young girls other benefits, like the chance to learn teamwork, experience victory, and practice good sportsmanship. Most important, I said, sports can give girls and women the confidence and independence to succeed in all aspects of life—a financial, emotional, and physical foundation on which the rest of their lives can flourish.

Despite my impassioned, and admittedly romantic and sentimental, diatribe, my students remained unconvinced. They accepted the fact that women do not have equal opportunity in sports, but they continued to question whether that even mattered. Most of these students worked to put themselves through college, so they had very little time for anything that did not further their educational or career goals. Practicality was crucial for them. They challenged me to provide concrete examples of what sports have done for women in the past. "Prove it," they said. "That's what you'd tell us!"

"Tell us about how sports can make a difference in the lives of real people."

"Anybody like me ever really make a living by playing sports?"

They were right, of course, and after that discussion I started looking for the evidence they demanded. I knew the statistics about the importance of physical activity, and I was well aware of the teamwork skills and confidence that sports provide. But my students wanted concrete historical examples of the ways in which sports have made a difference in women's lives. And not just the elite few but also, as they said, "women like us": athletes whose background and experiences mirrored their own.

It was this conversation, and my students' insistence that I make connections between sports and a definition of success that they could apply to themselves, that led me to the National Baseball Hall of Fame in the summer of 2003. As a lifelong baseball fan, I looked to this sport and the women who played it to find the examples my students had challenged me to uncover. To start my research, I visited the Hall of Fame's archives. While I was there doing preliminary research on women's baseball history, the library director, Tim Wiles, suggested that I look at the files of the All-American Girls Professional Baseball League. I did, and after several excited conversations about what I found, he encouraged me to seek out the women. From Wiles I learned that the AAGPBL had a players association that held a reunion every year. "You can go and meet them. They love to talk about their time playing baseball," he encouraged me. I was nervous about going and unsure whether my presence would be seen by the players as an intrusion, but the prospect of meeting the women of the AAGPBL won out, and I booked my ticket to Syracuse, New York.

I could hardly wait to get to that reunion. It was September 11, 2003, two years after the attacks on the United States. It was also, as I learned from my taxi driver, the day that actor and comedian John Ritter died. Ritter was young and his death had come as a complete surprise—a sad situation, for sure. But my cabbie seemed completely consumed by it. "How strange that it happened on this day of all days," he said. "This will be another 9/11 we will always remember." While I, too, was sad about the loss of John Ritter, I thought to myself, "Do we really need another reason to remember this day?" Now, as I look back on that day, I realize he was absolutely right. That was another 9/11 I will always remember. But this time it would be for the amazing experience I was about to have with the women of the AAGPBL.

Once the cabbie deposited me at my hotel, groggy from my early morning flight, I sat alone in the hotel restaurant worrying about how the former players would receive me. I had no idea what to expect. Would they ignore me? Would they be aggravated by my presence and my questions? I worked up a good level of paranoia and was about to retreat to my room when I felt a hand on my shoulder. I turned to find a tanned, athletic woman staring down at me.

"You here for the reunion?"

"Yes," I managed to get out, and before I could say anything else she had put her plate and coffee cup on my table.

"I'm Karen. Who are you?"

We talked for two hours about baseball, the AAGPBL, my work, and life in sports. Karen bought my breakfast, and then she told me to get some sleep since I looked "like shit." I left for my room to take a nap, and she went off to play golf. Turns out I had breakfast with Karen Kunkel (1952), former player with the Grand Rapids Chicks, advisor for the movie *A League of Their Own*, and a driving force behind the creation of the All-American Girls Professional Baseball League Players Association.[2] Not a bad start.

A few hours later, I entered the lobby only to find it full of women from the AAGPBL. They had just returned from a trip to the Baseball Hall of Fame in Cooperstown. I watched in awe as they interacted with their old friends from the league and with the scores of people waiting to get autographs. As I stood there taking it all in, a short, bouncy woman came up to me and asked, in heavily accented English, "Do you know where Jane is?"

Isabel "Lefty" Alvarez (left) and her "counselor" Jane Moffet. The AAGPBL reunion, Syracuse, New York, 2003.

Introduction

"Sorry, I don't know Jane."

And before I could introduce myself, she said, "Holy cow, there she is. Can you carry this?" and Isabel "Lefty" Alvarez (1949–1954) took off across the lobby with me (carrying a large suitcase) in tow.

Once we reached the other woman, larger and seemingly more confident in her surroundings, I introduced myself. Then Jane Moffet (1949–1952) asked Lefty, "Who's this?"

"I don't know," Lefty said. "She was just standing there and I liked her face."

I smiled, and Jane laughed, teasing Lefty about giving her stuff to people with nice faces. "You don't know her, what if she was a thief?"

From behind me another voice said, "I don't know, I think she has

Earlene "Beans" Risinger (left) and the author—my first AAGPBL reunion, Syracuse, New York, 2003.

a nice face, too." I turned to see a very tall, lanky woman. And thus Earlene "Beans" Risinger (1948–1954) joined the discussion. When I told her my name she said, "Ah, Kit Kat." I remained Kit Kat until her death in 2008.

"Jane," Beans went on, "you gotta admit she does have a nice face and a funny name. She must be OK. She could carry your luggage, too." With a belly laugh and a slap on the back, Beans walked away. The others followed, and I was left with Jane's and Lefty's luggage.

That was it—the moment I knew.

I walked outside and called home. "You know those times in your life when you experience something and you just know it is going to change you forever? That you will never be the same?" I tried to explain. "This is one of those times. I don't think my life will ever be the same." And it hasn't been. Those women—their stories, spirit, courage, determination, and friendship—continue to influence my life and my work. Seeing and talking to them sixty years after the league had ended, it was clear that this 9/11 would indeed be unforgettable for me. The lives of the AAGPBL players, both in and out of baseball, would provide the stories that my students, and others like them, needed to hear about women and sports. This book is my attempt to share those stories.

The history of the All-American Girls Professional Baseball League is well known. The popular 1992 movie *A League of Their Own* immortalized the women who played ball in the 1940s and 1950s. Numerous young people have repeatedly viewed this movie on cable television, making heroes out of the 600 women who helped to change the rules of sports for the rest of us. The players' 1988 recognition by the National Baseball Hall of Fame received national attention, and there are numerous books dedicated to the AAGPBL. The story of the league has earned its place in popular American history, and its focus on professional female athletes is no longer a shock to the gender sensitivities of the American public. Of course, when a story becomes this well loved and well worn, it risks becoming old hat. Indeed, some people claim that there is nothing of importance left to say about the league. Yet, beyond the image of Geena Davis sliding into home and the story of the glorious twelve years that the league was in operation, what do we really know about the women who played professional

Introduction

baseball? How do we talk about the broader impact of that moment in sports history, and how do we get at its deeper significance?

These are the questions that shaped my early research. In *Coming on Strong*, Susan Cahn suggests a way to begin answering them. She challenges sports historians to resist simply retelling the story of an athlete or the history of a sport. For Cahn, asking questions about the connections between sports, gender, and class opens new possibilities that she believes can help us better understand women's lives and experiences. And ignoring sports and their impact on the lives of women leaves a hole in our understanding. Cahn's use of oral histories and probing gender and class analyses allows her to examine the tension between the supposed "masculine" world of sports and women's participation in these sports.[3] Following Cahn's recommendation, this book examines the ways in which the AAGPBL changed the personal, educational, and financial circumstances of the women who played and how access to baseball defined the players' lives, especially after the league ended. Cahn led me to new questions: How did the women's experiences of playing professional baseball affect their lives after hanging up their cleats? Were these women, whom my students would happily identify as being "like us," shaped by their experiences as players in ways that can tell us something about the importance of sports for girls and women?

At the sixtieth anniversary reunion of the AAGPBL, I talked to players about the significance of their participation in the league—how their lives were changed as a result of their time playing professional baseball and what they felt was the significance of the league itself. Their answers varied because their experiences were unique, but without exception they told stories of the opportunities and profound changes that baseball brought to them personally. Each of the women featured in this book—Isabel "Lefty" Alvarez, Terry Donahue, Jane Moffet, Karen Kunkel, Delores "Dolly" Brumfield White, Jean Cione, Earlene "Beans" Risinger, Madeline "Maddy" English, Maybelle Blair, Katie Horstman, Shirley Burkovich, Annabell Lee, Mary Moore, Jean Faut, Audrey Wagner, Joyce Westerman, Helen Filarski, Norma Dearfield, Ann Petrovic, Elma "Steck" Weiss, Audrey Daniels, Dorothy "Kammie" Kamenshek, Marge Wenzell, June Peppas, Wilma Briggs, Helen Callaghan, Faye Dancer, Tiby Eisen, Jeneane DesCombes Lesko, Joyce McCoy, Helen

Smith, Jerre DeNoble, Betsy Jochum, Patricia Brown, Marie "Blackie" Wegman, Mary Pratt, Ruth Richard, Pepper Paire, Jacqueline "Jackie" Mattson, Jacqueline Baumgart, Janet "Pee Wee" Wiley, and Ruth Davis (bat girl)—had different stories, backgrounds and post-league experiences, but in every case it was the league and their time playing baseball that gave them the opportunities to grow and live as they did. The players represent diversity in class, region, educational attainment and nationality, but for all, no matter how it is defined, success was most certainly a byproduct of life in the AAGPBL.

Because of the popularity of the film *A League of Their Own*, the story of the AAGPBL is familiar to many Americans. The film focuses on the creation of the league during World War II. And the war did have everything to do with the league's formation. The Selective Training and Service Act of 1940 required young men to register for the draft, and two million men had joined the military by the end of 1941. That large number put pressure on every profession, including baseball. During the first year of the war, only four major league baseball players were called to serve in the military, but by 1945, 509 major league players and more than 3,000 minor leaguers left baseball to join the war effort. Almost 90 percent of major league baseball players served in some branch of the military during the war. And, of the 44 minor leagues that existed in 1940, only twelve survived the war years.[4]

From the beginning of the American war effort, owners, players, and fans expressed fear that the conflict could jeopardize baseball. After all, the U.S. entrance into the First World War had ended the 1918 baseball season on September 2, and only the armistice had saved the following season. Fearing that "America's pastime" was in danger, baseball commissioner Kenesaw Mountain Landis wrote to President Franklin Delano Roosevelt, inquiring as to the game's wartime status. The president responded on January 15, 1942, in what became known as the "Green Light Letter," which urged Landis to keep baseball up and running. "I honestly feel that it would be best for the country to keep baseball going," the president wrote, adding that he would like to see more night games that hard-working people could attend. Roosevelt noted that baseball could provide relief from the stress of wartime for at least 20 million fans, even though the quality of the teams might be lowered

Introduction

by greater reliance on older players.[5] As it turned out, major league owners found a different way of replacing those athletes-turned-soldiers, securing their profits, and keeping baseball fans in the stands.

Concerned about both the war effort and the future financial success of baseball, in 1943 Philip Wrigley asked his Chicago Cubs general manager, Ken Sells, to find new ways of maintaining attendance levels at both minor and major league ball parks. Aware of the success of women's softball throughout the Midwest, Sells suggested that the creation of a women's professional softball league might offset the loss of revenue. Wrigley agreed, and along with Branch Rickey and Paul V. Harper he established the All-American Girls Professional Softball League. Wrigley sent baseball scouts to amateur and semi-professional baseball and softball teams around the United States and Canada looking for talented female players. The scouts held regional tryouts, and if players made the cut, they were invited to attend the league's final tryouts in Chicago. In April 1943 seventy-five women from the United States and Canada arrived at Wrigley Field. Managers of each team were told to pick seventeen players to start; by the time the first spring training was over, each team would be cut to fifteen players. League play began on May 30, 1943, with four teams: the Rockford Peaches, the South Bend Blue Sox, the Kenosha Comets and the Racine Belles. For that first game, South Bend played in Rockford, while Kenosha played in Racine.[6]

The popularity of the league grew beyond anything Wrigley could have imagined. The teams were well received by fans in the four home cities, and attendance reached 176,612 for the 1943 season.[7] Because many of the previous attempts to put women on the baseball field had been made by promoters who wanted to make money off the spectacle, the quality of play had not always been good. Fans of the new league were amazed at how well the women played baseball. Enthusiasm and support for the teams spread beyond the original host cities. But it was not only the quality of play that made the league a success. It was also important that the league was founded during wartime. Going to the ball park was a popular form of entertainment, but with the travel limits the war placed on Americans, people tended to spend their leisure time close to home. Wrigley counted on this fact when he convinced others to invest in his idea of establishing a women's baseball league.

After two seasons, Wrigley and other owners believed the war was nearly over and did not see the continued need for the women's league. All of them, Wrigley included, began unloading their financial holdings in the AAGPBL. At this time, Arthur Meyerhoff, the league's advertising executive, bought control of the league and kept it going through 1950. These years after the war ended were in fact when the league saw its biggest profits.[8] In 1950, the remaining owners bought out Meyerhoff. The league then entered a period of decline that led its end in 1954. The decline was marked by an issue that had plagued the league from the beginning: How do you sell women playing a men's sport?

The league inherited this problem from women's softball. Before the establishment of the AAGPBL, softball was very popular throughout the Midwest. In 1939, an estimated sixty million fans watched softball games, which is ten million more than those who watched baseball. While both men and women played softball, women's games were more popular. But even though the game had been created for women as a socially acceptable version of baseball, in the popular press softball players were often portrayed as masculine, or even homosexual. At this time, lesbians were seen as the ultimate threat to respectable womanhood.[9] Thus, while capitalizing on wartime support for women stepping into men's jobs, Wrigley had to deal with the negative image of female softball players.

Wrigley countered that image with his own vision of AAGPBL players as "the girl next door, in spikes." He required the players to represent "the highest ideals of womanhood and healthy, wholesome, 'all-American' girls."[10] Regardless of their talent on the field or how much fans appreciated it, players had to be, first and foremost, feminine. And this wasn't just their image. Wrigley insisted that women in the AAGPBL live up to their billing as "nice girls."[11]

To ensure that the players maintained the image he desired, Wrigley demanded that Arthur Meyerhoff develop what he would call the "femininity principle."[12] Players were expected to follow the conduct rules or suffer fines. They also had to go to charm school at the Helena Rubinstein Cosmetics Company. There, they were taught how to put on makeup, get in and out of a car, put on a coat properly, enunciate correctly, and charm a date. The girls were officially forbidden to drink, gamble, violate curfew, wear shorts or slacks in public, or go out on dates alone without permission. Officials did everything in their power to represent the league and its players as simply "a colorful sports show," played by "feminine type girls with masculine skill."[13]

Because they realized what a great opportunity playing in the league was for them, players were willing to negotiate balancing their off-field feminine image and their athletic image on the field. By forcing the women to wear dresses and makeup, even while playing, Wrigley and the other league officials maintained at least the appearance of femininity, which successfully upheld society's acceptable role for women and kept the concerns about "manly women" at bay.

The acceptable image of femininity that Wrigley used to control the players included some very deep-seated assumptions about race. Despite the fact that African American women played softball, the league did not reach out to them. In segregated America, black and white men did not play together, and because most people believed that respectable white women needed protection from black men, it would have been unthinkable to include women of color in the league. African American women did play baseball, however. At least three—Toni Stone, Connie Morgan and Mamie "Peanut" Johnson—played alongside men in the Negro leagues. Scores of other African American women played the game, and on many different levels. But none ever played for the AAGPBL. Nor were they included in concerns over protecting the respectability of women. Arguably, African American women were those most in need of the kinds of benefits the league provided. They suffered extraordinarily during the Great Depression and did not enjoy the same opportunities as white women during wartime.

Although traditional notions of "proper white femininity" were, on the surface, upheld during the league's twelve-year existence, the mere fact that women played professional baseball circumvented the culture of masculinity that lay at the core of the game. Nothing challenges the presumptive dominance of masculinity more than female baseball players. After all, no major American sport has the same historical association with American manhood that baseball can claim. Women of the AAGPBL entered the world of professional sports and for years managed successfully to reconcile what society deemed feminine (and therefore acceptable) behavior for women with the masculine and physical qualities of baseball. But by the early 1950s, this was becoming a problem.

After Meyerhoff sold the league, individual franchise owners looked for promotional gimmicks to increase revenue. Some resorted to having their teams play exhibition games against men's teams. This put the league in direct competition with men, thereby altering the image of the women's league. That change in focus and the eventual postwar clash between women's presence on the baseball diamond and the mid-1950s conservative emphasis on home, family, and marriage finally forced the league to end operations in 1954. Thus, women's baseball became a victim of postwar conservatism and increasingly limited definitions of femininity.

Despite these issues and the ultimate demise of the league, the experience of playing professional baseball transformed the lives of the nearly six hundred women who played for the All-American Girls Professional Baseball League. In the succeeding chapters, the players' lives provide the lens through which the themes of financial benefit, travel, exposure to diversity, patriotism and, finally, the women's legacy are explored.

Chapter 1 examines the economic benefits of playing in the AAGPBL. Because education and economic security are inextricably linked, both subjects are discussed in this chapter. Each of the women discussed in this book used the money she earned in different ways, but the common thread that runs through all the players' stories is that this money gave them opportunities they would never have had if not for professional baseball. The fact that access to professional baseball furthered the education of many former players is an important piece of this puzzle. Formal education was not the goal of all players, and for some, like Lefty Alvarez (a player with a sixth-grade education), it was not relevant at all. However, for Beans Risinger, Dolly White, Maddy English, Audrey Wagner, and Katie Horstman, the ability to pay for an education was one of the most important benefits of their league experience.

The theme of Chapter 2 is travel and exposure to diversity. For players such as Lefty Alvarez of Cuba; Terry Donahue of Melaval, Canada; and Beans Risinger of Hess, Oklahoma, traveling through the United States and South America while playing baseball provided a view of the world they would have never had otherwise. In addition, because the league was founded at the beginning of World War II, many former players believe that their work in the league was as important to the war effort as Rosie the Riveter's. Doing their part to keep morale up and the national pastime alive during the war was, to some, the most important part of their baseball years. Chapter 3 discusses the players' military service and lifelong patriotism.

Chapter 4 focuses on the players' legacy. When one asks a former All-American about the legacy of the AAGPBL, without fail they will tell you that they made history. They provided a foundation for the passage of Title IX. Girls and women are better off because they played. Every player featured in this book understands the importance of that legacy, and it is that place in history that they most covet and are most willing to discuss.

Chapter 5 is titled "Life After: The Reconnection." For many of the women, the thirty-year separation after the league ended was difficult, while for others those years were happy and successful. All agreed, however, that once they were reunited in the 1980s, life began anew. This chapter focuses on the players' lives once they reconnected through the AAGPBL Players Association and examines the impact that the movie *A League of Their Own* had on their lives.

The final chapter, "The Next Generation," explores the connection between the All-American Girls Professional Baseball League and the current opportunities for girls and women to play baseball. Although circuitous, the path to women's baseball opportunities in the twenty-first century can be traced from the AAGPBL. Efforts to create leagues for women and to secure a girl's right to play Little League have met strong opposition, but the desire to play has fueled growth. At every phase in the process, individuals point to the historical foundation provided by the women of the AAGPBL.

In the conclusion, some assertions are made about sports history in general, offering new ways of exploring women's sports history. This final section also discusses the financial, personal, and professional effects on women in this period and discusses the long-term impact of former players on future generations of young female athletes, as well as American history in general.

It is my hope that the stories of these professional baseball players will inspire the casual reader but will also encourage other scholars to explore more fully the role of sports in women's lives and to begin using sports not only as a venue in which cultural, physical and recreational aspects of society are explored but also as a place for scholarly examination of class, gender, and work.

1

Independence

"All of life is a constant education."—Eleanor Roosevelt[1]

Writer Virginia Woolf famously claimed that all a woman needs to write is a room of her own and enough money to support herself.[2] Woolf was born into an elite British family and a world in which women were expected to be financially and emotionally dependent on men— first fathers, then husbands—and defer to the interests of male family members. Devoting herself to her art required autonomy. Woolf would no doubt be surprised to see herself referenced in a book about American women's baseball, but her argument is as relevant to the lives of female professional baseball players as it was to the writer herself. In order for the players to fulfill their dreams, they, too, needed self-sufficiency, a room of their own. And for them, that "room" was the baseball diamond. It was there that these women found independence, a sense of self-confidence, and their own money. And from this they were able to transform their lives.

Most of the women of the All-American Girls Professional Baseball League played baseball because they loved the game. But through the twelve-year existence of the league, the game also became the foundation for better, more fulfilling lives and careers. Playing professional baseball had lasting effects on former players, and most refer to the economic opportunities granted by the league as having the greatest impact. For these women, many of whom came from working-class backgrounds, good wages gave them a chance to fulfill lifelong dreams. That could mean reliable employment, and thus stability. Or it could mean access to higher education and a chance to have a career that they did not believe was possible before baseball. Players link these financial opportunities to the increased self-confidence resulting from their experiences in the league. This was a powerful combination. In fact, most of the six hundred women who played in the AAGPBL would agree that the educational and financial opportunities it provided, along with important lessons about self-reliance they learned during their playing days, provided the foundation on which their futures were built.

The chances that the ball players would eventually have access to higher education and well-paid careers would have seemed slim in the 1930s, when most of them were children. This was an era when most women did not work outside the home. Those who did worked in what are known as "pink-collar" jobs, which consisted of service work such as domestic service, clerical work and waiting tables. Those few women who were able to get a college education might become nurses or teachers.[3] These were low-paying jobs that allowed women very little opportunity for financial independence. Because these jobs were defined as being for females, they were reduced to a low level of social significance. The Great Depression only intensified the antagonism toward women who worked for wages. Even if they were the sole support for their families, they were accused of taking jobs away from men. When Norman Cousins, an American political journalist, was made aware that the number of employed women in 1939 was very close to the national (male) unemployment total, he quipped, "Simply fire the women, who shouldn't be working anyway, and hire the men. Presto! No unemployment. No relief rolls. No depression."[4]

Like other women of their generation, the AAGPBL players' lives were changed by World War II. When the United States entered the war after the 1941 Japanese attack on Pearl Harbor, all of America went to war—including the women. The most familiar image of women and work during World War II is that of the fictional character, Rosie the Riveter, whose powerful arm and fierce expression are still widely recognized. Rosie was created by the Office of War Information, which launched a propaganda campaign designed to make the idea of working outside the home in male-only jobs both acceptable and desirable for women.[5] With nearly sixteen million men in the military, women were desperately needed to fill the vacant positions. The campaign urged women to "Do the Job He Left Behind." Their country was asking them to fill those roles, so stepping outside the traditional roles was all

1. Independence

right—at least for a while. Rosie the Riveter became the most famous face of this propaganda effort. Before long, women were learning to operate welding machines, wield rivet guns, read blueprints, and drive and maintain railroad engines. Today, Rosie still represents the more than 400,000 women who served in all branches of the armed services during World War II and approximately six million women, both single and married, who filled war industry jobs.[6]

Like the Rosies, the ball players replaced men who had gone off to war, enjoying the possibilities for well-paid work that had been unavailable to generations of women before them. But what happened to the players after the war ended was different from what happened to the Rosies. However, because scholars writing about women's labor during the war have discussed only the challenges, triumphs, and disappointments of women factory workers, they have missed this story.[7] And it turns out that the difference matters.

The story of the Rosies ends with the war. Despite the popular image, most of these real-life workers were not middle-class women entering the workforce for a short, patriotic stint; rather, they were primarily working-class women looking for better-paying jobs. At the beginning of World War II, 25 percent of American women held jobs outside the home; by the war's end, this number had only risen 11 percent.[8] Many of these women wanted to keep their jobs after 1945, but that would not happen. At the war's end, women were expected to give up their positions to returning veterans. And they did so. Nationally, women's employment in industry dropped significantly. Those who were fortunate enough to find alternative employment did so at a much lower wage level. Women who had earned an average of 85–90 cents per hour during the war were forced to take jobs that paid 45–50 cents after the war ended. In Detroit, the percentage of women working in the automobile industry fell to 7.5 percent from 25 percent, and in Los Angeles only 14 percent of the women who had worked in aircraft plants during the war still held jobs by the middle of 1946.[9]

Many working-class women, whether married or not, moved back into low-paying "women's jobs." There were few other options. Higher education did not hold out much promise. During World War II, the majority of college students had been women, filling places left by men, but this changed in the postwar years. Men returning from the war had unprecedented access to college through the Servicemen's Readjustment Act of 1944, or "the GI Bill," and the influx of male students pushed women out. The percentage of women among college students dropped to a low of 35 percent by 1958.[10] Many left school to get married, and most of those who stayed in school were not expected to be preparing for a career. Lynn White Jr., president of Mills College, proposed in *Educating Our Daughters* that the curriculum for female students should prepare women to "foster the intellectual and emotional life of her family and community."[11] Female students taking liberal arts and professional courses were also encouraged to take classes in interior decoration and family finance. Throughout the 1950s, the male president of all-female Radcliffe College told his incoming freshmen students that their education would make them "splendid wives and mothers, and their reward might be to marry Harvard men."[12] Even for women who did earn a college degree, there were few employment options. In 1957, 70 percent of working women held clerical, assembly line, or service jobs; only 12 percent held a professional position, while 6 percent were in management.[13] The story of women and work in the 1950s is one of loss and often desperation.

The story of the ball players in the postwar era is strikingly different. The most obvious dissimilarity that the AAGPBL players experienced was that, unlike their counterparts in the factories, many of them were able to keep their jobs after the war's end. In fact, the league saw its greatest growth after the war. Many of the league's host cities developed junior leagues for young girls in the postwar era, and in 1948 the league acquired franchises for teams in Peoria, Illinois, and Muskegon, Michigan. In the first three years after armistice, teams attracted more fans than they had during the war, ranging between two and three thousand fans coming to a single game. A July 1946 double-header in South Bend attracted an estimated 10,000 people. AAGPBL attendance reached a high during the 1948 season, when the ten teams then in existence attracted 910,000 fans.[14] The league lasted until 1954. Thus, while some female ball players retired once World War II ended, an even larger number continued to play baseball.

Another significant difference in the league's story was the amount of money these girls, predominantly from poor and working-class families, were able to earn. Players in the AAGPBL made only $45–$85 per

20

week on average, with a few stars earning closer to $100. But even the lowest paid among them made a great living compared to the jobs they held before their professional baseball careers. And, although far less than what male professional baseball players earned at the time,[15] the money these women earned from baseball was a sizeable sum for women earners in the 1940s and 1950s. "I know it doesn't seem like much money now, but I made more money than my father, and that money changed my life and the lives of my family," recalled Maybelle Blair, who played in the 1948 season.[16] Her story is very much like those of other players. Isabel "Lefty" Alvarez (1949–1954) also talked about the effect of her high income on her family: "Holy cow, I made a lot of money. I used to send some to my mother in Cuba. It helped her and made her proud that I had such a big income in America."[17]

Helping their families was only one way ball players used their incomes. The one usage they talk about the most was what Dolly Brumfield White called "one of the most important aspects of [our] league experience": access to higher education.[18] Because they earned relatively high salaries while playing baseball, many players were able to afford a college education, an opportunity most would not have had otherwise. This was another area where the experiences of the league women differed from those of the less well-paid Rosies. The fact that the AAGPBL lasted for over a decade may also have contributed to the difference. AAGPBL women could rely on salaries longer than their industrial counterparts and take advantage of the expansion of higher education in the 1950s.

And they did take advantage. Former players earned associate degrees, bachelor's degrees, and even PhDs, MDs and law degrees. Some became doctors, lawyers, teachers, librarians, or college professors. A study by Carol Pierman reports that 35 percent of the AAGPBL participants went on to earn a college degree. A survey of about one-third of the six hundred former players put the number slightly higher: just under half claimed to have received at least a college education. In either case, the final tally was much higher than the national average of 8.2 percent of women in that era. Pierman also shows that 14 percent of the AAGPBL participants went on to earn a graduate degree, with five becoming physicians and two becoming dentists.[19] As a result of these opportunities, many of the players, including Maybelle Blair,

Maybelle Blair at the 2015 Baseball for All national tournament in Orlando, Florida. Maybelle was a star even to girls as young as 10; they knew the importance of what she and the other women did on the diamond.

Earlene "Beans" Risinger, Dolly Brumfield White and others, moved from being uneducated and working class to educated and middle class. Because they earned enough money to pay for an education, their lives—financial, professional, and personal—were changed forever.

For certain players, the financial benefit of playing in the league did not manifest itself in a college, or even a high school, degree. Rather, it allowed them to identify and achieve their own version of success, a different kind of education. Jane Moffet (1949–1952) put this idea especially well. Jane was a catcher and utility player who played many different positions during her four years in the league. She went on to earn a college education, becoming a teacher and later a principal, but she also understood the larger significance of what women learned from playing ball.

> To me, education means more than just what you learn in the classroom. It is a lifelong process. But we have to start somewhere. We have to have the chance. I realize now that baseball is the reason I had the chance at an education, not just the formal kind, although that is true, too, but the lifelong kind. I learned to learn because of baseball. For many of the girls, they did not get a college education or even a high school education, but they got an education as ball players and that was what *they* needed.[20]

A final way that the players' stories differed from those of the Rosies lies in their attitudes about independence, which were built on the league's greater financial and educational opportunities. Maybelle Blair was one of the many players who were proud of their self-sufficiency: "I was the first woman in charge of a division at Northrup Airlines and that not only made me proud but gave me independence. Nothing was more important than that."[21] This desire for autonomy is most obvious in the players' attitudes about marriage. Women of the league were less likely to get married than other women of their generation. While national marriage rates were high in the postwar years, the 1997 National Baseball Hall of Fame questionnaires filled out by former players document that 82 (42 percent) never married.[22] Answers to the question about whether they were married solicited some telling responses. One woman replied, "Hell no." Another player claimed to be "happily single," and another wrote, "No way." In a personal interview, Terry Donahue (1946–1949) was asked what she thought about the women who were married and had to live apart from their husbands during the war. "Well, if I had to have a husband," Terry responded, "I'd just as soon he was in another state."[23] Playing professional baseball made it possible for women to make alternative choices about marriage and family.

The story of the AAGPBL adds to our understanding of women and work in the post–World War II era, reminding us that the story of women's participation in the war did not begin and end with the Rosies. The ways in which the league experience differed in its high wages and persistence into the 1950s made a big difference for those women. And that difference shaped their lives even after the league ended. The rest of this chapter will explore the three crucial themes of financial stability, education, and independence in the lives of Delores "Dolly" Brumfield White (1947–1953), Earlene "Beans" Risinger (1948–1954), and Isabel "Lefty" Alvarez (1949–1954). Their stories illustrate the cultural, regional and ethnic differences among the players and demonstrate some of the many ways that participating in the league affected those who played.

Delores "Dolly" Brumfield was born in Prichard, Alabama, on May 26, 1932. She was the oldest of three children. Dolly liked and played most sports.

> I did not like paper dolls, that's what the girls were playing and they would cut out these little paper dolls and have these little tea sets and that never appealed to me. I'd rather have the beanpole and do the pole vaulting over the neighbor's bushes or around the school were big ditches and we'd pole vault across the ditches. Those were the things that were more interesting to me and of course we always had the basketball games and the football games and baseball games and that was the environment in which I grew up.[24]

But baseball was in her blood.

The Brumfield family lived near an elementary school and a block away from a junior high school, both of which had baseball diamonds. "We were on the school ground most of the time," Dolly explained in an interview. "I primarily grew up on the school playground." Her early baseball experiences are not unlike those of other AAGPBL players. There were no girls' baseball teams, so if she wanted to play, she had to have the courage to play with the neighborhood boys. Dolly would not be denied. She was called the "tomboy of the neighborhood, but it didn't matter," she recalled.

Dolly was a good athlete. When she played baseball, even the boys knew she was among the most talented on the field. Nearly always chosen first, Dolly was a valued team member. But it was her play with local shipyard workers that ultimately drew her to the AAGPBL. Men from the yards began using the junior high school baseball field after their workday ended, and Dolly was nearly always present to watch. They let her play catch with them and eventually allowed her to play in some games. She so impressed the men that they told her about a women's baseball league. According to Dolly, in 1946 the shipyard workers read in the *Mobile Press Register* about the AAGPBL going to Pascagoula, a town near Dolly's home, and they encouraged her to try out. They even offered to drive her.

> So some of the guys went to my parents and wanted to take me to the tryouts, but my mother said—no, if you think she should go, I'll take her, so one April afternoon in 1946 we borrowed my grandmother's car because daddy had to go to work in our car and she took me out of school and we drove to Pascagoula, Mississippi where I actually tried out. After I had done all the things Mr. [Max] Carey asked me to do, the hit, throw, run business, he asked me how old I was. It wasn't until I had done all those things he asked me how old I was, so I told him—I'm thirteen and I'll soon be fourteen, but he said—we don't take the girls that young, and he went over to talk to my mother and he said—Mrs. Brumfield, we don't take the girls this young, and my mother said—I don't want you to take her. So that was my tryout.

Despite her young age, Dolly impressed league officials with her play. They encouraged her to continue working on her skills and to try out again when she was older. Returning to the Mobile area, Dolly joined a softball team made up of women from a local military base. League officials kept up with her play, and near the end of the 1946 season she received a letter from Carey. She was told to report to Havana, Cuba, for spring training in 1947.

Later, Dolly remembered that the homesickness hit very quickly, but once she arrived in Havana, the focus on baseball made everything easier for her. After spring training in Cuba, Dolly was sent to the South Bend Blue Sox. In the next year, the league expanded to ten teams and split into two divisions. In 1948 Dolly was traded to the Kenosha Comets in Wisconsin. She played for Kenosha through the 1951 season, when the team folded. She spent the 1952 season with the Fort Wayne Daisies. Her last season in the league was 1953, which found her again playing in Indiana for Fort Wayne.

Dolly's father was an auto mechanic, and college had never been an expectation for his children. In fact, because she was a girl, her father didn't think she should be educated. But, like many of the other AAGPBL players, Dolly understood the importance of education to her own life and independence. She knew that if she was going to get an education, she would have to pay for it herself. During her playing days, she saved money and, with her mother's and grandmother's help, went to college during the off seasons, continuing after her playing days were over. She remembers the importance of the life choices that the league provided.

> Because of the league, because of the opportunity I had to play in this baseball league, I was able to make money. I was able then to get my education and that was so important to a lot of the girls that played in the league. If it had not been for that opportunity there would not have been a college education for many of us, certainly not for me.

As a person who was always interested in sports and physical activity, Dolly attended the Alabama College for Women (now the University of Montevallo) in 1954, majoring in physical education. Her goal was to teach physical education and coach girls' sports. Alabama did not have varsity sports for women in those days, but Mississippi

Delores "Dolly" Brumfield White—always ready to sign an autograph (photograph by Cami J. Kidder).

did. In 1959, Dolly left Alabama to attend the University of Southern Mississippi, where she received her master's degree and then a doctorate in physical education in 1969. The AAGPBL women had few sports-related opportunities once the league ended, but, like many other players, Dolly was able to parlay her experience of playing professional baseball into a career of teaching, coaching, and inspiring others.

Dolly's first teaching job was a two-year stint in Shaw, Mississippi, followed by seven years at Copiah-Lincoln Community College. Dolly was an adventurous woman, and knowing that she could play baseball with much older and more experienced players, and do it very well, gave her the confidence to take chances. She was always looking for a new challenge and increased opportunities to coach women's sports. After her time in Mississippi, Dolly decided to interview for a new job in Monroe, Louisiana. During the car trip she stopped in Arkadelphia for gas.

> I told my friend, "I kind of like the looks of this place. I'll see if they've got a job." So my friend dared me to call. I went to the telephone booth on the corner and looked up Henderson State. I told them who I was, and that I was passing through, and that I was looking for a job in my field, and asked if they had a job in my field. The secretary said, "Yes we do." She invited me to meet the president. I talked with him and he took me to the P.E. department and showed me around. He said, "If you're interested in the position, send us your paperwork." I got home, sent in paperwork, and within a week I got a call offering me the job. I've been here ever since.

Dolly retired from Henderson State College in 1994 after teaching for forty years. She is clear that without the chance to do the thing she loved—play baseball—her life would have been very different and far less fulfilled. She emphasizes the ability to choose, to make her own decisions in her life.

> It was so important to know that we could have done anything. Some of us used the money for school but for others, it was a way to help, not only ourselves, but our families. Many of the girls were very poor before playing in our league.

Dolly is also clear that her successes in life are the result of her love of baseball and the opportunity she had to play it professionally.

The economic impact of the AAGPBL is most apparent when looking at those who had the furthest to climb. Much like Dolly White,

Earlene "Beans" Risinger was able to build a successful life and professional career because of the opportunities that baseball afforded her. As was the case for Dolly, baseball served as a guiding force for Beans from an early age. The game not only made a career possible but also allowed her to commit herself to teaching and coaching the girls who followed.

Beans was born in Hess, Oklahoma, on March 20, 1927, to Lizzie and Homer "Soupy" Risinger. The Risingers were sharecroppers who, despite Soupy and Lizzie's best efforts, often had a hard time making ends meet. Beans' father worked at a local gas station and her mother grew food for the family. Still, the family, like most in Hess, was poor. When asked about the impact of the Great Depression on her childhood, Beans said, "Depression? What Depression? We used to laugh and say we never even knew there was a Depression in Hess. We blew in depressed."[25]

Although the financial struggle and stress of poverty made life difficult, the Risinger family found ways to survive, both financially and emotionally. Baseball, Beans remembered, was a huge part of that effort. Soupy Risinger played first base on the sandlot team from Hess, which was a source of pride for Beans even fifty years later. They played against local teams, especially a team from Altus, a slightly larger town than Hess and less than twenty miles away. Unlike Dolly's town experience of being the only girl in her neighborhood to play baseball, in rural areas it was common for both boys and girls

Earlene "Beans" Risinger.

to play baseball with their families and friends. Beans was no exception. Some of her earliest and fondest memories were of playing with her father.

Soupy taught his daughter to play catch, and Beans quickly learned the game. She loved it. By the time she was six, Beans was a regular on Sunday afternoons down at the cow pasture, playing ball with her dad, her uncles, and her cousins. She became an integral part of those weekly games. In addition to learning the game of baseball on those Sunday afternoons, Beans and her family were able to escape for a few hours from the financial hardships of the Great Depression.

While baseball gave Beans a great deal of joy and brought her closer to her father, she still had to face financial realties as she got older. There were few employment or educational prospects in Hess during the 1930s and 1940s. "After graduation, here I was with no future. We [Beans and her siblings] never even thought about going to college, because there was no money for college. We were so poor that we couldn't afford the newspaper."[26] For two years after graduating from high school, Beans worked in the cotton fields. It did not take long, however, before she was given the chance of a lifetime.

Always a reader, Beans Risinger stopped every day at the local grocery store, where the sympathetic grocer let her read the Oklahoma City newspaper without charging her. In the spring of 1947, she read an article in the sports section about two women's professional baseball teams that were playing a spring exhibition series in Oklahoma City. The article also claimed there would be tryouts for any young woman interested in playing professional baseball. Excited by the prospect, Beans sent a postcard to the sportswriter who had written the story. He forwarded her card to the All-American Girls Professional Baseball League Management Corporation in Chicago. She quickly got a letter back inviting her to the tryouts in Oklahoma City.

Unsure and admittedly a bit afraid, Beans needed (and received) encouragement from the men with whom she played baseball, including her father. Male support for girls and women playing sports was unusual in the 1940s, but, like Dolly Brumfield White and her shipyard workers, Beans remembered that it was crucial. Her uncles, brothers, and father saw and always fostered her athletic abilities. They helped her practice and perfect her pitches, and they allowed her to take hours of batting practice. When the time came, they supported her desire to leave the family to play professional baseball. With their blessings, Beans set off for Oklahoma City to try out for the AAGPBL.

Because of her strength, athletic ability and what she called "a great fastball and a 'nickel' curve," Beans was offered a contract to play for the Rockford Peaches. Neither Beans nor her family had the money for the train fare to Illinois, so she went to the bank in Altus, where she applied for and received a loan to pay for the ticket. But Beans had spent her whole life working alongside, playing baseball with, and living with her family. "So, when I got off the train in Chicago, rather than find the train to Rockford, I found the train to home." In hindsight, she laughed at her homesickness, but at the time, she remembered, "getting back home was all I could think about, not the loan or whether my family would be disappointed in me. I just needed to get home."[27]

Once back in Hess, Beans returned to picking cotton. Fortunately, the AAGPBL did not give up on her. In 1948, Beans got another letter from the AAGPBL, asking if she would be interested in trying out with the Springfield Sallies. This time she was ready. By then, the pitching style used by the AAGPBL had changed to an overhand throw, and pitchers with Beans' talent and experience pitching overhand were desperately needed. Once again, Beans' family encouraged her to try out for the league. With their support she boarded the train, now bound for Springfield, Illinois. And this time she got there.

Beans became a member of the Springfield Sallies. In the 1949 season, the Sallies became a touring team, part of a minor league that was used both to recruit and to develop young players. Those who had played for the Sallies prior to 1949 either were sent to other teams or became part of the touring team. Beans went to Grand Rapids, Michigan, to play for the Grand Rapids Chicks. From 1949 through 1954, the last year of the league, she played for Grand Rapids. "That team was my family," she said. "Grand Rapids became my home." Given Beans' love for and comfort in Grand Rapids, it is not surprising that she decided to stay there when the league came to an end.[28]

When Beans picked cotton in Hess, she made "about fifty cents a hundred pounds. That worked out to maybe $12.50 a week pulling cotton. It was seasonal, but you had to do it." As a professional baseball player, however, Beans made "$60–$70 a week. That was a lot of money and I thought I was rich."[29] Because of the money she made while play-ing baseball, Beans was able to go to X-ray school at Butterworth Hos-pital in Grand Rapids after the league ceased operating. Once her training there was over, she began working in an orthopedic surgeon's office. She worked for the same surgeon until her retirement in 1991. Beans never married and, like so many of the former players, prided herself on being able to remain independent throughout her life. "A lot of people say the league really made their lives. Well, it did for me. It got me out of the poverty in Oklahoma all the way to Grand Rapids."[30]

Beans Risinger achieved a great deal as a result of her time in the AAGPBL. She was a very talented athlete who dreamed the baseball dream and ended up playing in the All-American Girls Professional Baseball League. When asked, "What did playing in the AAGPBL mean to you?" Beans smiled and said,

> Well, everything. It meant everything. Possibly I would still be in Hess, Okla-homa, which isn't a bad place to live if you have a profession and can drive some place to work. At that time, I had nothing, and now I feel satisfied with my life and I am a very happy person.[31]

A lot of women have stories similar to those of Dolly White and Beans Risinger. For many, formal education was an important byprod-uct of playing in the AAGPBL. But, as Jane Moffet reminded us, formal education wasn't the only kind that league players received. Perhaps one of the best examples of this fact is Isabel "Lefty" Alvarez. Her ear-liest memories are of baseball in the streets of El Cerro, a section of Havana. "I was the only girl that played ball in my neighborhood and a real *pilla* [rascal]," she said in an interview in 2011. Despite being the only girl, she was a leader, and often the winner of those kids' games. She loved to "be out on the street playing pelota, playing marbles, climbing trees or stealing mangos and lemons off trees." It didn't matter what the game or sport was—she excelled. But baseball was her first love, and playing the game on the streets of her neighborhood garnered attention. As Lefty explained, "The neighbors gave me the title of La Pilla Del Cerro because I was always out on the street playing baseball and showing off."[32]

The street version of baseball was somewhat different from what we recognize as baseball today. Lefty fondly recalled how the children made their own balls: "We collected old cigarette boxes from the garbage, tore them into strips and wrapped them into a ball shape."[33] They also used their hands for bats. It was not until she began playing for the Cuban women's team that Lefty got her first baseball glove. Yet those games on the streets of Havana were crucial in honing her baseball skills.

Although Lefty was a good baseball player and an all-around good athlete, she never thought about a career of any kind, especially not as a ball player. But her mother, Maria, dreamed that someday Lefty would go to America and live out the life that she wanted for her daughter, a life that was out of Cuba and away from the limited opportunities available to the working class in Havana. In 1947, baseball presented itself as a way to achieve that goal. Lefty remembered that it was not unusual for girls to play baseball in Cuba: "There were more boys on the streets playing ball, of course, but we all played. Baseball was our game."[34] Maria's determination, coupled with Lefty's talent, landed Lefty a spot on an organized baseball team for girls in Havana.

This opportunity was created without Lefty's knowledge. Maria talked to Raphael de Leon, a wealthy Havana beer and wine merchant who was asked to sponsor and develop women's baseball in Cuba, either by Max Carey, who had many contacts in Cuba, or by Wrigley Company contacts.[35] Lefty was unsure how her mother found out about this newly formed women's baseball league, but she recalled, "One day I was down in the streets playing ball with my brother, and my mother came and she took me to an organized baseball team in Havana." That was where she first met de Leon. Despite her youth and inexperience, and with the help and encouragement of her mother, Lefty attended training camp. "You're a ball player, my mother would tell me, you're a ball player. Never quit," Lefty remembered. "Be persistent."[36]

Lefty recalled de Leon saying she was a natural athlete, one who clearly had the dedication and determination to compete.[37] He not only recognized and recruited her talent but also bought Lefty her first baseball glove. Even though she was only fourteen, Lefty made the team. The Cuban players were provided with dresses, uniforms similar to those of the AAGPBL. They trained every day, and on weekends players were housed at de Leon's ranch. He fed them and taught them the AAGPBL version of baseball, all in preparation for the league's 1947 spring training trip to Havana.

1. Independence

The Havana team played the AAGPBL team in a number of exhibition games in the spring of 1947, and after one such game de Leon took Max Carey, the league president, to the Alvarez home. Lefty remembers being there as Carey explained the AAGPBL to her mother, including the chaperone system, the pay, and the rules by which Lefty would have to abide upon joining. She would have to return to Cuba each year in the off-season and would only be allowed to return to the United States with a signed contract. Since Lefty was so young, Carey required her to wait a year before joining the league, but he allowed her to accompany other Cuban players and two AAGPBL teams on a tour of Central and South America during the winter and spring of 1948–1949. Lefty enjoyed playing in the exhibition games, but her life changed forever when she boarded a plane for the United States in the spring of 1949.[38]

In May 1949, Lefty was just fifteen, spoke no English, and had no real idea of what to expect as she prepared to leave Cuba for the United States. When asked if she was afraid when her family took her to the airport, she said, "No, I was not sure if my mother was crying or not. I didn't look back. I just picked up my bag and walked up the steps to the airplane and a new life." Lefty did not have any memory of her father's or brother's last words to her—only her mother's: "Never give up." It was with her mother's confidence, the glove given to her by de Leon, a borrowed suitcase, and the naiveté of a fifteen-year-old that Lefty boarded that plane.[39]

Lefty played in the league from 1949 to 1954, first with the Chicago Colleens, then the Fort Wayne Daisies, then the Kalamazoo Lassies, and finally back to Fort Wayne. She sat out the 1952 season because her contract was lost in the Cuban mail system. The year away from baseball provided Lefty with some distance, a chance to mature a bit, and the realization of just how much playing in the league meant to her. "I missed baseball very much," she said, "but mostly I missed my teammates."[40] She returned to the league for the 1953 season as a Kalamazoo Lassie. Later that season she was traded back to Fort Wayne. She played until the spring of 1954, when she injured her knee, spent a month in traction, and then underwent surgery. Lefty never returned to uniform after the injury.

Lefty decided to stay in Fort Wayne when the league ended rather than go back to Cuba, but she did not follow the path to college that Dolly and Beans had taken. Lefty had only finished the sixth grade before she headed to the United States to play baseball. There were several reasons why Lefty had so little formal schooling. As a young girl in the 1930s and 1940s, Lefty was expected to attend school, but only to learn the basics: reading, writing and math. Most Cuban families at that time did not have the same educational goals for daughters that they had for sons. And, for most families, there was even less expectation that girls would have a career other than that of wife and mother. But for Lefty there were other issues as well. School work itself petrified her. She remembered:

> In school, I panicked and was so nervous. I couldn't wait until it was break time so I could go out and play ball.... [At the time] I didn't really understand why, but now I see I just couldn't do school. I was afraid, and now I think they would call it a learning disability.[41]

Acquiring a high school education in the United States became important to Lefty—not because she wanted a profession or even a college degree, but because she knew that having only a sixth-grade education was a detriment to finding a well-paid job. "Everywhere I applied for asked about high school," she remembered. "You had to circle the number of the highest grade completed and I knew that I could only circle 6, so that held me back." After the league folded, Lefty enrolled in night school. But despite the support of friends who drove her to class, Lefty could not go through with it. She hid in the bathroom every night rather than attend. One day her friends came early to pick her up and saw her feet under the stall door. She had to tell them the truth—that she just could not face going to school.[42]

It was during this time that Lefty began to accept that maybe an official education was not the kind of education she should have or even needed. "My mother said it was okay, I could be something without it." And, although finding a job she liked that paid enough to live on was not easy, she did "keep swinging." While working in a number of service jobs, including a waitressing stint at a bar called the Nine Mile Place, Lefty kept applying to General Electric. All of her friends worked at GE and liked it, so Lefty decided that "this GE must be a good place to work." She continued to apply until they hired her in

1. Independence

1962 on her fourth try. To Lefty, the job at General Electric allowed her to reach an important goal: permanent employment doing the kind of hands-on work she enjoyed. "I never wanted an office job; I'm not made for that. I am more mechanically inclined—I can do anything with my hands, like work on a car, plumbing or carpentry." Lefty, who never married, supported herself with her job at GE until she retired, making a better living than most without a formal education.[43]

For Lefty, success in life did not depend on formal education. Instead, as she is quick to point out, the league provided her with what she needed to be an independent woman. "I am here, in America," she explained, looking back on her life years later. "I have money. I retired from a good job and can buy what I want. That is all true because I played in the AAGPBL." And it wasn't only her opportunity to immigrate and have access to a well-paying job that the league provided. Being in the league, playing professional baseball, gave her the education she needed. It taught her how to fight, how to lose and how to win, and, most important, to never "stop swinging."[44]

If we use the broader definition of education provided by Jane Moffet, that "we have to learn to learn" and that it is a "lifelong process," the number of examples of those who benefited educationally from their time in the AAGPBL grows. There is Joyce Westerman (1945–1952), who faced family disapproval when she decided to join the league. Like so many who had suffered through the Great Depression, her parents were leery of this "job," and with good reason. Society made it clear that there were real jobs, respectable ones, that were acceptable for women; baseball was not among them. But Westerman persisted and, having attained that goal, went on to a life of blue-collar employment and independence.[45]

Sports are too often seen as simply a game—a leisure-time activity—where little that is serious takes place. Women "play" sports, but they "work" in factories. But for these ball players, as for others who have worked in the sports arena, historically and today, expertise on the playing field was indeed a job. In the 1940s and 1950s, it benefited women and their families in much the same way that factory work benefited other members of the working class. Clearly the number of women who played professional baseball during World War II is much smaller than the number of women who worked in factories, and it is possible to argue that baseball did not employ enough men or women to place it at the center of a discussion of working-class women's history. But given that the story of the ball players was so different from that of the Rosies, it raises some important questions about the history of women and work in the 1950s.

Playing professional baseball had a lasting effect on former players, and, as the examples in this chapter illustrate, many women point to the league's provision of economic opportunities as its greatest impact. The examples are numerous, but the point is the same. As Beans Risinger, Dolly White, and Lefty Alvarez all attest, the financial effects of the league were long lasting. By their own admission, without the opportunities afforded them by baseball, they would not have achieved the level of professional success they ultimately enjoyed.

In 1943 a group of young women was given the chance of a lifetime—the opportunity to earn a good salary by playing professional baseball. Those experiences were transformative in many ways beyond their education and their working lives, as we shall see in subsequent chapters.

2

Travel and Exposure

"As the traveler which has once been from home is wiser than he who has never left his own doorstep, so a knowledge of one other culture should sharpen our ability to scrutinize more steadily, to appreciate more lovingly, our own."

—Margaret Mead[1]

Those of us fortunate enough to travel, to see places, cultures and struggles that are very different from our own, benefit greatly from that experience. We see with our own eyes how people live and work in difficult situations; it makes us realize how different we all are from one another, and how to appreciate those differences. Travel can enlighten a person regarding differences in culture, food, fashion, religion, politics, and so much more. Unfortunately, travel is not readily available to everyone. In the 1940s and 1950s, the working and middle classes rarely experienced its benefits. The Great Depression, gas rationing, and wartime travel restrictions made traveling especially difficult. Without what Mary "Sis" Moore (1950–1952) called "the golden opportunity of travel"[2] provided by the All-American Girls Professional Baseball League, most of the league's players would not have had this chance to grow personally and appreciate both a wider world and the one in which they played and lived.

This advantage was especially important in the post–World War II period, which was characterized by affluence for much of American society, as well as a population boom, but also by a socially conservative mood that guided women back to more traditional roles and kept America racially segregated. The Cold War added greatly to a politically conservative climate in the country. The fear of communism guided foreign policy, and conformity and conservatism characterized the

37

social norms of the time. Such compliance was even encouraged in popular advertising. Advertising in women's magazines changed from encouraging American women to "join the war effort" by taking war production jobs to pushing the latest kitchen appliances and telling women how to be good mothers. Dr. Benjamin Spock, author of the popular book, *Baby and Child Care*, told mothers that they should devote themselves to the full-time care of children, and popular culture depicted marriage and feminine domesticity as a primary goal for American women.

But there was a stirring of change in this period as well. After the war, segregation and inequality within the United States were brought to the forefront as over a million black soldiers who had served in the military during World War II demanded equality once they returned home. President Harry Truman appointed a special committee to investigate racial conditions in America and later issued an executive order ending racial segregation in the military. By 1954 the civil rights movement was under way, pushing the country to begin thinking about issues of social justice and equality.

Like most Americans of the time, the AAGPBL players were patriotic and proud of their service to the country during the war. But women of the AAGPBL were also shaped by witnessing the racial inequities in the American South and the poverty and cultural difference in Latin America, and by simply living and playing with women from different backgrounds. Although few of these women would consider themselves social activists, the sights and experiences to which they were exposed helped them to become more tolerant and open-minded. And some trace a commitment to social justice and equality back to their time traveling with the league.

Travel was a prominent part of players' lives in the AAGPBL. Women left their homes, many for the first time, to join their teams. And as players they traveled across the country, usually on buses. It was not uncommon for teams to travel overnight, play a double-header, and then get back on the bus and head to the next ball park. Most of the league's games took place in the Midwest, but exhibition games during the pre- and post-seasons were often more wide ranging. There were games in the American South, the northeast, and even Canada.

Players traveled the longest distances during spring training. From

2. *Travel and Exposure*

1943 to 1948, spring training in the AAGPBL was very different from that of major league baseball, which has each team hold separate training. All of the women's teams trained together, making the yearly relocation of talent easier to accomplish.[3] League personnel could also assess the players and make changes to the team rosters, ensuring the equal distribution of talent. The AAGPBL had to adhere to the same travel restrictions as everyone else during World War II, so having the players in one location was also practical. Each year, the location of spring training changed. During the league's first year, training was held in Chicago at Wrigley Field. In 1944, spring training took place in Peru, Illinois, and in 1945 it was back in Chicago at Waveland Park. After the war ended, seasonal travel restrictions were lifted, so from 1946 to 1948 the league embarked on a more ambitious training schedule. Spring training was held in Pascagoula, Mississippi, in 1946; Havana, Cuba, in 1947; and Opa-locka, Florida, in 1948. From the 1949 season onward, spring training camps were organized by the individual teams as a way to save money.[4]

Most of the spring training trips were notorious among the players for overwhelming heat, bad accommodations, and long days. Dr. Harold Dailey, director of the South Bend Blue Sox, declared that the Mississippi training camp was the "worst mess I ever saw." According to Dailey, there were no real diamonds to play on, and the housing was "alive with roaches and bugs of all kinds."[5] The players' experience in Cuba was very different, however. More than two hundred players and league personnel went by train to Miami and from there flew to Havana, where they were housed at the luxurious Saville-Biltmore Hotel and played at the fantastic Gran Stadium de la Habana.

Spring training was followed each year by a series of exhibition games, which provided a real game atmosphere in which coaches and managers could make decisions about players before the season started. After two weeks of spring training, the teams paired off and traveled from the training camp to their home fields, playing exhibition games along the way. Once home, they opened the regular season. These exhibition games were important to the league, increasing its visibility across the country and leading some of the league's best and most memorable players to join up. But the exhibition games were often very difficult for the players. They suffered through exhausting travel schedules, poor playing facilities, and at times even worse housing arrangements. Again, the situation in Cuba was very different, in part because of the reception the teams received from Cuban baseball fans. According to Harold Dailey:

> The Americanos became the rage of all baseball-mad Cuba. Hundreds turned out to see them practice. And no less than 50,000 wildly enthusiastic fans watched the round-robin tournament which concluded the training program. In the opening game of the final series between the Racine Belles and the Muskegon Lassies, the crowd numbered over 20,000 and gave convincing proof that Cuba had taken girls baseball to heart.[6]

Spring training in Cuba was a highly successful endeavor for the league and those players fortunate enough to attend. League officials, such as advertising executive Arthur Meyerhoff, wanted to build on that success. They realized that in order for the league to continue, they would need to improve their ability to attract talent, create greater visibility, and increase profits.[7] Meyerhoff hoped that adding a post-season international exhibition tour would provide all three benefits to the AAGPBL.[8] The first post-season tour went to Cuba in 1947 and consisted of two AAGPBL teams, the "Atlántidas" and the "Nortenas," aptly named for that trip. The Cuban team was called the "Columbians." League officials scheduled forty-four games that fall, a tour that would have taken the women through Central America and into South America.[9] Possibly due to a lack of funds, however, the exhibition never made it out of Cuba.

One reason for the planned tour was that Meyerhoff and AAGPBL president Max Carey hoped to expand the league into Latin America. In mid-January 1948 they tried again. A number of league players and two teams from the Latin American Feminine Basebol League (LAFBL) played exhibition games in Maracaibo and Caracas, Venezuela. They played nine games in all, each bringing in an average of 7,000 fans. A game that pitted the combined American and Latin American players against a team of Venezuelan girls drew nearly 12,000 people.[10]

With one successful Latin American tour under his belt, Meyerhoff quickly embarked on another. Just 6 weeks after the 1947–1948 winter exhibition, many of the same AAGPBL players rejoined the Cuban teams for another tour in Cuba and Puerto Rico. And then, from January to March 1949, Carey and Meyerhoff teamed up for the more ambitious tour that they had originally planned in 1947. Two AAGPBL

2. *Travel and Exposure*

teams and a group of Cuban players competed. The two teams from the AAGPBL were called the "Americanas" and the Cubans were the "Cubanas." Only league players played on the Americanas teams, but in order to equalize the talent, some of the Americans were moved to the Cuban teams.[11]

The tour began in Guatemala, after which it moved to Nicaragua.[12] From Nicaragua the teams went to Costa Rica. While in Costa Rica, the teams were honored by the U.S. ambassador and his wife, who attended their game at the National Futbol Stadium. From there they traveled to Balboa, Panama, where the teams had a very busy schedule. In one day, they rode 50 miles, played a game in Mt. Hope Stadium, and, despite being exhausted, spent time at the Panama Canal. After touring the canal, they were "back to the barracks, supper and another ball game. Mickey (Migdalia Perez) hurled for the Cubans and Beans (Earlene Risinger) for the Americans. Game was good and so was crowd."[13] The teams then moved on to Venezuela. The tour was supposed to include Santo Domingo in the Dominican Republic and go back to Cuba, but it does not appear that those games took place. The tour was a financial drain on the league, so it was cut short. After 1949, the league did not go back to Cuba or South America, but the impact of those trips was widespread and long lasting.

Most women who played in the AAGPBL would agree that without the league they would never have had the opportunity to see so much of the world. Regardless of where they started from, in nearly every case playing professional baseball exposed the players to a world that they could never have imagined. In turn, their lives were different, richer, and, according to some, simply better. Looking at the travel experiences of some of the players, it is possible to see what that experience meant to them at the time, and how it affected their lives once their playing days were over. The stories of Norma Dearfield (1949–1950), Mary Moore (1950–1952), Helen Filarski (1945–1950), Ann Petrovic (1944), Katie Horstman (1951–1954), Joyce Westerman (1945–1952), and Jane Moffet (1949–1952) provide a sense of the challenges, excitement, and long-term impact of travel on players.

Few of the women who played for the AAGPBL had been exposed to much of life outside their hometowns, churches, and families, so

41

the opportunity to travel changed their lives profoundly—even if that travel was only by bus and in the middle of the night, as Norma Dearfield remembered it. Dearfield was born in McKeesport, Pennsylvania, the second of five children. Like so many of the other AAGPBL players, she was active in sports from an early age.

> When I was very young I always had a tennis ball, always, and I was throwing it into the house or anywhere and catching it. I just liked playing ball and the Christmas when I was about twelve years old, I asked for a baseball glove and my mother told me that girls don't get baseball gloves and I said, "then I don't want anything for Christmas, if I can't have a glove, I don't want anything," so needless to say, I did have this glove and it was the same glove I played—my dad bought me a good glove at the time which surprised me, but it was the same glove that I still have today and that I played in the league with.[14]

The combination of her persistence and her parents' support gave Norma the opportunity to play baseball. The gift of that glove represented acceptance from her father and an acknowledgment that she could and should play baseball. Her father became her coach and supporter, as well as the person who traveled with her to the tryouts for the All-Americans. "My father went with me for a few days and when he realized the league was ok, he gave me his blessing. My father and that glove took me a long way," Norma recalled.

And Dearfield did travel a long way from her small town in Pennsylvania. While the memories of the time spent traveling, often on long bus trips, were not always pleasant, the bottom line for her many years later was that she got to do it at all.

> We were in like thirty-eight states. We went through the Midwest and out as far as Texas, Oklahoma, all in through some of the western states, South Carolina and Georgia, almost all of them. I have little pennants from every state and I had one wall filled with every city that we played in because we played in several cities in one state when we would get there. We traveled all night. [Mostly] by bus, it was like a school bus and not a very comfortable one, but we would travel short distances some of the time and sometimes as long as two or three hundred miles to the next city.... Oh, there were a lot of people and they were very receptive to us. Several times we had several thousand people there for the games.

As she recalled, the players did not have time to do much else besides playing baseball during their travels.

2. *Travel and Exposure*

We really didn't have time to do a lot of sightseeing or anything like that, but we had some time during the day, but most of the time it was just play ball, take the bus to the next town, go to bed because you didn't sleep good because you traveled all night and then you had to get to the Laundromat to wash the clothes that you had. You only had a little small suitcase and you weren't allowed to take much of anything.

But Dearfield did not seem too upset by her inability to sightsee while on the road. "After all we got to play baseball!" she said. The AAGPBL "gave me the chance to play professional baseball, travel and make life-long friends with people I would have never known if not for baseball." The importance of travel for Norma can be observed in her determination to remember every place that she visited, buying a "little pennant" as a symbol of how far the league took her.

Mary "Sis" Moore pointed to her travel experiences as the most cherished aspect of her time in the league. Unlike Norma, Mary did remember sightseeing.

The travel around the United States and Canada was fantastic. I mean, just think, here we were traveling all around, seeing our country, playing baseball, meeting people, and all of this with a salary and all expenses paid. We were kept on the move because many of the games were one night stands. But in some places we got a chance for sightseeing, like going to Radio City Music Hall in New York and visiting Coney Island. Playing baseball in Griffith Stadium in Washington, D.C., was great but even greater than that was playing in Yankee Stadium, where I got to meet Casey Stengel, Billy Martin, Phil Rizzuto, Yogi Berra and Joe DiMaggio.[15]

Moore was originally from Lincoln Park; as a girl, she played baseball in the fields around her house. She was from a working-class background, as her father was a tool die maker for the Cadillac division of General Motors, and Mary is clear that without the league she would not have seen much of the country. Like other players, Mary began playing baseball with an older brother and other boys from the neighborhood:

I played out in the fields with the boys [in] Lincoln Park you know, well it wasn't very populated. There were a lot of fields out there where we lived at that time. We were like the only house in fact; there was one other house on the lot on one side of the street and maybe one or two on the other side. So there were a lot of fields out there and we would take them and cut the weeds down

43

and make our own ball field. And of course if you get it to the right field we were out and we didn't have enough players but it was always something to go out to the field with the boys. I had an older brother that had a paper route, *Detroit News*, and it was a weekly paper. And so I would help him on his paper route to earn money. So I was the one who always would come up with bats and balls and the equipment. So if the boys wanted to play ball or any sport be it football, basketball, they had to come get me first.[16]

Mary was not above using manipulation and buying her way into the games, as long as she got to play. Unlike other girls of her time, Mary was lucky enough to have a part-time coach who taught her the fundamentals of the game. This happened because Mary was friends with a young woman who babysat for Eddie Lake's children. Lake played in the majors for eleven years, the last five for the Detroit Tigers. He often joined the neighborhood kids in the vacant lots that served as

Left to right: former players in the dugout—Mary Moore, Helen "Nordie" Nordquist, Toni Palermo, Jackie Baumgart, Joyce Westerman, Pinky Alverson. Put me in, coach! (photograph by Cami J. Kidder).

baseball fields, hitting balls to them. Mary said of that experience, "His presence had a great affect on me. That was 1947 and 1948. I had no idea at that point that there was a women's league, but thanks to Eddie's help and playing baseball with the boys, I learned the game and learned to love the game."

Mary graduated from high school in 1950. Since there were few employment options available for young women at that time, one of her teachers put her in touch with Doris Neal, another former student and a player in the AAGPBL. Mary met with Doris, who invited her to a local gym to practice with some of the players from the Detroit area. It was there that Mary met Helen Filarski, who played for the South Bend Blue Sox. The two became lifelong friends. Filarski took Mary to her team's spring training in South Bend, and they gave her a tryout. South Bend liked her play but said the team couldn't use her. Instead,

AAGPBL reenactors talking to an original player—Mary Moore (photograph by Cami J. Kidder).

they sent her to the Chicago Colleens, one of the two traveling teams. Mary agreed to join the Colleens and went immediately to Chicago, where she found that she was one of 100 players trying out for just 30 spots. She did not become a Chicago Colleen, but the Springfield Sallies chose her to play second base. After a successful 1950 season with the Sallies, Mary went back home and got a job in an auto parts factory. She was drafted by the Racine Belles for the next season and planned to join the team at its new location in Battle Creek. Then, in January 1951, Mary was involved in an accident on the job and lost two fingers to a punch press. Her throwing hand had been damaged, and she was afraid she would never play again.

True to her stubborn nature, Mary decided to go to spring training anyway. Unfortunately, fear that she would be further injured kept the league from allowing her to play. Toward the end of the season, however, Battle Creek called her back because of injuries to other players. Despite her own injury, Mary played most of that season as well as the following one, until an ankle injury finally ended her baseball career. She tried to play in 1953, but her ankle was not healed enough, so she "quit baseball and went home."

Even though Mary's career was cut short, she believed that the impact of playing in the league was long lasting.

> The things we learned from playing baseball in the league will stick with us for the rest of our life. I just can't say enough about the experiences we had in the traveling and learning to get along with people, working as a team, learning responsibility, and just everything I think helped almost every one of us in our life and in our time after the league. Playing in the league was one of the greatest experiences in my life, and I wouldn't trade anything in the world for the time we played baseball.

While the whole experience was transformative, Mary Moore especially credited her time traveling with the league for making her the person she is today. "I would never have seen the country," she has said, "but maybe even more importantly, I would never have seen and gotten to know the diversity that is this country." It was her interactions with her varied teammates and all of the disparate "people I would never have met around the country" that mattered most. "That exposure made me, all of us, better, just better." When asked how it made her better, Mary had a hard time narrowing down the ways baseball had changed her, made her better: "Friendships, and you know not be, not be afraid to be out in public, playing in front of 2,000 people you aren't bashful. Of course the discipline was always there and that always helps too. And just ... everything you know?"

Ann Petrovic's story of travel illustrates how even a single incident can be both devastating and transformative. Born and raised in Aurora, Indiana, a town of around five thousand people, Ann was the youngest of nine children, five of them brothers. As was true of many other players, her brothers got her into baseball. In 1944 she tried out for and was chosen by the league to play for the Kenosha Comets and then for the Minneapolis Millerettes.

Left to right: Ann Petrovic (former player), Phyllis Smallwood (associate member of the AAGPBL-PA), and Mary Moore (former player). The players will sit and sign autographs as long as there are people in line who want them. They are clear about their place in history and welcome the opportunity to share it with their fans (photograph by Cami J. Kidder).

Being from a small town and a large family, Ann never thought much about travel before she joined the AAGPBL. But, like Mary Moore, some of her most important memories came from the experience of travel, of being able to "really feel what it meant to experience the world." It was the chance of a lifetime, "and we got that from baseball," she has said.[17] But one incident in particular stayed with her. As a young girl, she had experienced the war only through stories and newspapers, until one road trip.

> We did long road trips and while playing for Minneapolis, I can remember this one—we were getting on this train, not the bus, the train, and it was a troop train, I'll never forget it. Fifteen girls got on that train with these servicemen and it was something else. I was fifteen years old, so I just got in a corner and watched what was going on. The guys were wanting you to write to them and asking when they go overseas and stuff like that. They were giving out addresses and talking to you and stuff, but it was some experience and I really enjoyed that.[18]

Petrovic and others who traveled during the war saw up close, the faces of war. In those moments a larger world was brought into focus.

For Norma Dearfield, Mary Moore, and Ann Petrovic, the opportunities to see and experience the diversity of the country were among the most positive, life-altering aspects of their time in the league. These women pointed to the lessons about tolerance and understanding they learned as a result of traveling the country with players from different regions and cultures. As a result of the closeness and sense of camaraderie that developed during those difficult days of travel, the players learned firsthand how important exposure to new and different things was to their personal growth. For others, however, there were harder lessons to learn. One of the most difficult was about racism. For Katie Horstman, the experience of seeing how diverse her own country was meant being confronted with inequality and unfairness.

A native of the small town of Minster, Ohio, Katie Horstman was the youngest girl of six children. Like so many of the other players, Katie's baseball story begins on a neighborhood field with her older brothers. Whenever the rest of the kids played baseball, she did, too. She started to play on the Catholic Youth Organization softball team in Minster in the fifth grade, and at 16 she was invited to tryouts for

Katie Hortsman. No matter what the competition is, it is always important to win (photograph by Cami J. Kidder).

the All-American Girls Professional Baseball League. Katie was chosen by the Kenosha Comets and later remembered that she "proudly signed a contract for $50 a week" to play for the 1951 season. From her first day in the league, Katie had many new and often challenging experiences, but she was also grateful to have "learned so much more about the world, about life" than she would have in Minster, Ohio.

Katie started at Kenosha but was traded to the Fort Wayne Daisies during the midseason, playing for them until the demise of the league in 1954. A natural athlete, Katie was a star player in the league and participated in the 1954 championship series. When the league ended, she joined several other players selected by former Daisies manager

Bill Allington to play in a national touring team known as the All-American All-Stars. The team played about a hundred exhibition games, each in a different town, and mostly against all-male teams. "Ten or eleven of us, including Bill, would pile into his Studebaker station wagon and Joanie Berger's sedan with a few bats and balls, gloves and we'd drive," she explained. The team played in one city, traveled 300–400 miles, often sleeping in the car, and then played another game. "It wasn't easy, but we just loved playing baseball."[19] The all-stars' booking agent, Mat Pascale, preceded the team and arranged the games as well as the advertisements and publicity. "Sometimes we would ride through town on a fire truck. We'd hold up signs about the game and the driver would blow the sirens. It was a way to get people to the games. It worked too."[20]

It was during her days traveling with the Allington All-Stars that Katie's most memorable experiences took place. They often played in less than favorable conditions. At one point they played in a dust storm in Kansas and in a near tornado at another location. But by far their most difficult experience was in a small South Texas town. It was 1954, the year the Supreme Court struck down legalized school segregation in the *Brown vs. Board of Education* case.[21] The civil rights movement had begun. But Katie, having grown up in a small Ohio town and playing with the all-white AAGPBL, had little awareness of segregation or racial discrimination. Then she went to Texas.

> The bookie scheduled the games, so we never knew who we were playing. We just played ball against the men and that was it. In this town the team happened to be a black team. In Texas at that time, whites did not play ball with blacks. We couldn't find the ball park, so we asked the sheriff where the ball park was. He asked why we wanted to know. We told him we were playing and Bill's attitude was "we are playing and that is it. No matter if we have a war." The sheriff said we cannot play that team. I was sitting in the back seat and asked, "Why not?" He said, "Well, they are black." And I said, "I'm from Ohio, who cares?" We went further down the street and asked someone else where we should go and they told us. We found the ball park; it was beautiful, music playing. It was great. The sheriff along with 5 other cop cars followed us. They pulled their guns and the things they said to the black men, I hate to say. But they threatened them and did not let the game take place. That was scary. I had no idea about segregation. I was from Ohio.[22]

Katie still remembers the shock she felt at the racism she witnessed, explaining that it helped to "form my adult views about race.

50

2. Travel and Exposure

People are all the same. I saw firsthand what happens when they aren't treated that way." While she is aware that racism was and is everywhere, this example of widespread segregation and blatant racism was eye-opening for her. "That experience above all stuck with me all these years. I guess I'm glad I had it." In her life since the league, Katie Horstman has tried to share that lesson. "Seeing the world, seeing that it was different outside Minster, Ohio, and not always better," she has said, "made it possible for me to believe even more strongly in fairness" and, as a teacher and a coach, "to demand it for myself and my girls."[23]

Many players remember being affected by the racial politics of the southern United States, but most of the memories they have focus on other aspects of the huge cultural differences they faced in that

Left to right: Former players Eileen "Ginger" Gascon, Joyce Westerman, Noella "Pinky" Alverson, and Lucella Ross. San Diego, 2013 (photograph by Cami J. Kidder).

region. Most of the ball players were from the Midwest, and for many, like Joyce Westerman, life in the southern states was completely foreign. Like most Americans from outside the region, she initially subscribed to the stereotype of white southerners as racist, ignorant and backward. That image was complicated, however, by the AAGPBL's travels in the South.

Westerman was born in Kenosha, Wisconsin, and raised in a small farmhouse with no electricity or running water. She had not experienced much of the world until she joined the league. Her first spring training was in Pascagoula, Mississippi.

> I remember going into the barracks—we were at an army base—opening the door and turning on the light and cockroaches running everywhere, you know. And we used to call it Cockroach Boulevard and something else you know. It was something else. We slept with the lights on but that was something else. But our managers at that time went deep sea fishing, and they came back with this [fish] and he cooked it outside on a fire. That was the best fish I ever ate in my life. That was quite an experience.

During the exhibition tour that followed, Westerman saw a different side of southern life:

> We played games with this other team which gave us the practice and people could see what kind of ball we played. And in many places the people there were so great you know. That one place, I think it was in North Carolina, the guy took us out on a cruise—he was a very rich man, you know—he took us out, I got pictures on the boat where we went out on a cruise and stuff like that. But we were in parades and stuff, it was fun. We used to kind of laugh amongst ourselves, we're not nothing you know we're just ball players. It was a great experience.[24]

Not only did she see the American South, but Westerman was also able to recognize the diversity of the region. It was about the cockroach boulevard, but also about the excitement of going on a cruise; it was about the racism that Katie encountered, but also about the welcome the women received as ball players. Playing in the South allowed the players to challenge regional stereotypes, both for themselves and for others.

Regardless of where they traveled within the United States, AAGPBL players were deeply affected by their experiences. Those who simply left small towns, rode a train for the first time, managed their own money and, even if for only a short time, witnessed life outside their comfort zones gained experiences, insights and strength from playing professional baseball. But for those who experienced international travel, the impact was even greater.

For some of the players, travel meant coming to the United States. The All-American Girls Professional Baseball League included a number of players (at least one-third) from Canada. For Audrey Daniels (1944–1951), who was from Winnipeg, Manitoba, leaving Canada was an experience in and of itself. She remembers her first trip away from home as her most vivid memory ("You know, one of those that you just never forget?"). She had never been more than one hundred miles from home. She had not even ordered from a menu and eaten a meal out.

> I was just about as green as the grass we were going to play on, you know. I had never had any experience being away, so it was a pretty exciting experience for me to join the other players from western Canada and get on the train in Winnipeg and head for Chicago. [I had] never been on a train before and it was nerve-wracking for me you know, you want to do the right thing and everything is new to you and I don't think I slept much that first night on that train and the first sun-up I looked out and saw the wonderful rolling hills of Wisconsin go by and it is a memory etched in my mind forever, those wonderful rolling hills and green grass. Everything I did—I was a little bit nervous about everything and when we had breakfast on the train I just didn't even know what to order because I had never been out. Seeing the waiter with this white towel over one arm and a silver coffee pot in the other hand, I was just baffled by it all. It was just over whelming to me, but we headed out and I guess most of the girls going were in the same position as I was.[25]

After she arrived for the tryouts, that sense of newness, and also of connection to the other women, continued: "I remember on a hot day [in Chicago] I had this pleated woolen skirt on and I was just about melting, but you met these girls and they were from all over the U.S. and Canada and you realized that they were in much the same spot that I was," she explained.[26] Daniels was "out of her league" when she first stepped on that train from Winnipeg, and perhaps again when she stepped into the Chicago summer wearing a wool skirt, but, as she pointed out, many of the girls were equally nervous, and out of that nervousness came friendship, family and a whole new way of seeing and living in the world.

Travel to the United States was just as nerve-wrecking for Lefty Alvarez. When she arrived in Chicago from Cuba it was early spring, and because she had never been to a cooler climate, she arrived without a coat. Fortunately, the host family assigned to her by the league met her at the airport with a coat and, as she remembered, "a warm smile."[27] The climate, however, proved to be the easiest thing she had to overcome. Because Lefty spoke very little English and was much younger than most of the players—only fifteen at the time—she was quite isolated and often lonely.

Lefty, however, made a big impression on many of the players. Katie Horstman remembered meeting her for the first time in Fort Wayne, Indiana:

Left to right: Katie Horstman (former player), Maybelle Blair (former player), and umpire Perry Barber signing autographs at the Louisville Slugger Museum at the International Women's Baseball Center's First Women's Baseball Symposium, 2014.

2. Travel and Exposure

As soon as I got there Max Carey had me pitch right away. He wanted to see my arm. Well, I had a pretty good arm and I was very accurate and I pitched and pitched for at least thirty minutes batting practice and Lefty Alvarez was picking up the balls and giving them to me and she was talking and I couldn't understand her and I thought, "what kind of a language is she talking and what am I getting into?"

She kept saying, "are you tired, are you tired, are you tired?" I thought, "gosh" and I finally turned around and asked somebody because I couldn't understand her and they said she was saying, "are you tired," and they said she was from Cuba. I said, "Cuba, where's that?" I had no idea. I really paid attention to the history lessons after that.[28]

Meeting a foreign player who spoke a different language was certainly an eye-opening experience for Katie. For Jane Moffett, the recruitment of Cuban players was also significant. It broadened her worldview and gave her an understanding of cultural difference. And she became close friends with Lefty Alvarez, which made all the difference for the young Cuban. While Lefty was eventually paired with other Cuban players, which helped her social isolation, Jane Moffet was the person who became one of her best, and most trusted, friends.

Jane herself joined the league almost by accident. A New Jersey native, Jane grew up in a family of sports fans, but, like most women of the time, she had few opportunities to play sports. During high school she did play field hockey and basketball, and after high school she attended East Stroudsburg University in Pennsylvania. During her freshman year a friend asked her to go with her to a women's baseball tryout. Her friend had read about the tryouts for the AAGPBL in an advertisement.

Jane had never played baseball and had no interest in trying out for the league, but she agreed to go to support her friend. During the tryouts, Jane began helping out by hitting and throwing. The scouts liked what they saw and offered her a spot in the league. She gave them her name and address but never expected anything to come from the offer. But in May 1949, Jane received a telegram from the league with instructions to report to Michigan; her train ticket would be forwarded. Jane's friend who had taken her along that day did not make the cut.

Jane's freshman year in college had been her first time away from home, and now the league was asking her to travel, alone, to Michigan. She called home to explain what was going on to her parents. Fortunately for Jane, her father answered the phone, and he supported the adventure. Jane promised to write once she got to Michigan. The next week, Jane finished her finals, "packed my one suitcase and walked a mile and a half to the train station." That train ride was her first trip away from the East Coast. "I must have asked the conductor ten times or more, 'How much longer do we have to go?'" After eight hours they reached Chicago, where Jane transferred to a train headed for Muskegon, Michigan, which arrived at 2:30 a.m. Jane remembered that the station was almost empty and there was no one there to meet her. The conductor on that train lived in Muskegon and his shift was finished, so he offered to drive Jane to her hotel, where she spent the night. Jane did not have a phone number for the league contacts, so the next morning she asked the hotel desk clerk to get in touch with the Muskegon Lassies. He was familiar with the team and called them. An hour later, the chaperone arrived and took Jane to the ball park. "So far my trip had not been fun, but I hoped it would get better. Not so. It got worse."[29]

Once she arrived at the field, Jane met the manager, who asked what position she played. "I don't know. I never really played baseball before," was her answer, and, as Jane remembered, "he looked at me very strangely." The manager then asked Jane about her glove and spikes, and she replied, sheepishly, "I don't have any." The manager instructed the chaperone to take Jane to a sports shop and buy her a glove, two bats, and a pair of cleats. According to Jane, things did not improve much after that. She was sent to Chicago to the Colleens, one of the league's traveling teams, to get more training. She arrived at a small North Side hotel, registered, and took a "very old elevator to the third floor." As she approached her room, she could hear the roar of a passing train and thought to herself, "This is most certainly not the Ritz."

She opened the door to her room and the "four girls already there looked at me like I was the Jolly Green giant. They started talking to each other in Spanish. I didn't even know what they were saying. I turned around and went back down to the desk clerk to tell him I was in the wrong room." He assured her that she was indeed in the right room and said, "You teach them English, they teach you Spanish." He did promise that another girl who spoke English was going to be in their room, too. That new ball player was Doris "Cookie" Cook (1949–1953), whom Jane would later room with in Kalamazoo. The "four mysterious Spanish-speaking strangers" turned out to be the new Cuban ball players who were joining the league: Mickey Perez (1948–1954), Mirtha Marrero (1948–1953), Ysora "Chico" Castillo (1949–1951), and Lefty Alvarez. In spite of the language difference, they all became very good friends.

Jane's education about cultural differences continued throughout her playing days. After ten days of spring training with the touring teams, she was assigned to the Springfield Sallies. During the 1949 tour they traveled "26,000 miles playing exhibition games across the country." Much like Mary Moore, Jane had not seen much of the country. "The opportunity to see this country, to experience what life was like outside New Jersey or Pennsylvania, was so valuable, and baseball did that for me, for all of us." In 1950, Jane returned to the Sallies and made a second tour to different places in the United States and Canada. In 1951 and part of 1952, Jane played for the Kalamazoo Lassies. During the 1952 season she was traded to the Battle Creek Belles. After that season Jane quit baseball and concentrated on her education and career.

These experiences greatly influenced Jane's teaching career, during which she taught high school and then spent 23 years as a high school principal: "I brought to my classrooms what I saw, what I learned during that time. It was easier to understand different ideas because I saw that people were different, some were poor and some were rich. Some were really good ball players and some were not. Some were even Cuban [said with a laugh]. I would never have met those Cubans sitting in New Jersey."

Meeting "those Cubans" was an important event in Jane's life, and Lefty Alvarez became a lifelong friend. Even today, it is Jane whom Lefty looks to for guidance and security. At the 2004 reunion in Kalamazoo, Lefty checked into the hotel and told the desk clerk, "I need to be beside Jane Moffet, she's my counselor." Unsure exactly what to say, the clerk agreed to the room assignment next to Moffet. Hours later, when Jane checked into the hotel, she was assured that her room was indeed "next to her patient." With a hearty belly laugh common to Jane, she responded with "Hell, I didn't even know Lefty was coming."[30]

For many of the players, the trip to Cuba for spring training was the only foreign travel experience of their lives. Marie "Blackie" Wegman's

(1947–1950) memory of the Cuban trip conveys a sense of adventure that many of the players would recognize:

> I still remember we left in April [from Cincinnati] and took a train to Louisville. There was a train coming from the West and a train coming from the East and they met in Louisville. There was an iron railing there and all these girls came off both trains and met at this railing. We were shaking hands ... and Dot [Mueller] and I looked at each other and said, "hey this looks like it might be fun." Then we got on another train and went to Florida. Then we flew from Florida to Havana. It was evening and when we got over the University of Havana, I can still remember the pilot circling the field so we could see where we were going to play.[31]

Blackie's excitement about playing ball in a new place is apparent in the joy she showed while retelling that memory, reveling in the details of every step of the journey.

For many players, however, the Cuban experience had its downsides. They were there during an exciting and unstable moment in Cuban history. The Cuban Revolution would hit the country in July 1953, just a few years later, and the AAGPBL witnessed the rumblings that preceded the upheaval. Political demonstrations in Havana led to concern for the players' safety, especially during the May Day celebrations, a labor holiday that was important to the revolutionary movement. For most players, the vivid memories of their time in Cuba dwell on the escapades they enjoyed, their anxieties about cultural difference, and the pride and excitement they felt in how they were received as players.

For some of the players, the life-altering experiences of being in Cuba happened off the baseball field, where the reality of cultural differences challenged them profoundly. This was true for Joyce Westerman. Because of her small-town upbringing and admittedly sheltered view, Joyce "had a lot to learn about the world."

> I had 3 sisters and 4 brothers and my mom and dad and we lived in that little house that did not have any running water, we didn't have any electricity, and we had a potbellied stove to heat the house, and we'd have to carry the water in from the cow tank and also [to] take a shower we had to heat the wood over the fire and stuff like that.... Well, then as I grew up, we went to a one room school with one teacher, actually the teacher taught my mother. She graduated from that school and I graduated from that school with the same teacher, from 8th grade from that school. So that in itself was an experience. I had played a lot of ball at school and stuff but then as I grew up and I graduated from high school

when I was 17, and you couldn't get a job till you were 18.... Finally, by the time I was 18 I got a job at Nash Motors in Kenosha making airplane engines. I was making a dollar an hour.[32]

During her childhood Joyce rarely had the opportunity to travel beyond her small town or encounter people very different from herself. This would change when she joined the league.

It was while she was employed at Nash Motors that Joyce saw the Kenosha Comets play and decided to try out. She made the team, but while she was elated, her family was not (at least at first).

> I went to spring training for tryouts and then found out that I made the cut and I would be going to Grand Rapids. I was so excited to have a contract to play baseball. My mom and dad were not sports people, and they never told me I couldn't play but just weren't sure. Well my dad was making $50—well $40 in the plant. I was going to make more than my dad, my contract was for $55.[33]

In 1945 Joyce Westerman became a Fort Wayne Daisy. She had a long career with the AAGPBL, playing until 1952. However, her first experiences of travel were not easy ones, and her small-town upbringing made it difficult to understand and accept cultural differences.

> That [the trip to Cuba] was quite a thing. My first airplane ride and first of everything and that was a lot of fun, I mean. But I wasn't too crazy about the food over there. So I learned to say leche, that's milk, so at lunch time they would have ham sandwiches always—good ol' American you know, with milk. So I kind of liked that. But they had fried bananas and powdered eggs and stuff I didn't much like.[34]

Although she was uncomfortable with the cultural differences, Joyce's description of her time in Havana reveals excitement and a sense of fun and adventure in addition to wariness regarding her surroundings.

> Well actually it [the game] was very much the same. But oh, the fans, yeah yeah. They were something else. Actually we drew more people over there than the minor leagues did, so that was really interesting you know. And being in the hotel and that, and walking on the streets you had to be with somebody all the time. And then we had May Day over there and you couldn't go out of the hotel you know, because it was just too dangerous. It was kind of comical ... we had the long rope that went down from like the 3rd floor and it had a basket on it and we would lower that and the guys downstairs would go and get us some cokes. And then we'd pull it up.... I remember that. And then going to Sloppy Joe's and meeting the gals there. Well it was a place where you could get a drink and something to eat. I guess they used a lot of, what is it they use over there to

drink? What is that drink? Rum, they have a lot of rum and stuff. Well, I wasn't a drinker so they had coke and stuff, never was one to ... never had a drink in my life.[35]

Although she was asked directly about her memories of playing the game in Cuba during an interview, Joyce stayed on that subject only briefly, quickly returning to her preoccupation with her experiences off the field. The political unrest made an especially strong impression. The safety of the ball players was always a concern for the league, even when traveling in the United States, but in Cuba during May Day celebrations they were sequestered in their rooms. For many such as Westerman, experiencing political and social unrest anywhere, especially in another country, was scary. But for her and most of the AAGPBL players, that fear turned to amazement at what they experienced because of baseball.

Westerman wasn't alone in being concerned about the political turmoil and the dangers it produced. During events like the May Day celebration or the unrest that spilled out onto the streets, the chaperones were charged with keeping the girls safe. Helen Campbell, a former Marine and new chaperone, traveled to Cuba with the league in 1947. The lure of visiting Cuba was one reason she took the job when it was offered to her by Max Carey. Upon arrival at the Biltmore Hotel in Havana, the players, with their managers and chaperones, were met with the excitement of Cinco de Mayo celebrations and a dearth of food at the hotel.

> The girls on the upper floors tied bed sheets together and dropped them out of the windows so the vendors could tie baskets with stuff in them. We tried to get all that from them because we had heard bad things about the Cubans gardens and there was no way they could prepare that food or even wash the fruit. We had a chore right from the start.[36]

The experience of cultural difference and political instability was powerful and shaped women's memories years later. But the pride they took in playing ball was always there too. For Joyce Westerman and Helen Campbell, the experience of being in a foreign country was overwhelming, and the cultural differences and political unrest made a huge impact. Baseball almost seems to disappear from the story. But as far as Terry Donahue (1946–1949) was concerned, it was all about baseball.

Theresa "Terry" Donahue (left) getting her marching orders from Jane Moffet (right). Both were on the committee to plan the spectacular reunion cruise that set sail in 2008. AAGPBL reunion, Grand Rapids, Michigan, 2004.

For Terry, who was from Melville, Saskatchewan, Canada, the trip to Cuba was just another step in a longer journey. Moving from Canada was not "too difficult, but I did miss home, my parents. But Cuba?!" Terry's trip to Cuba gave her what she called one of her best memories in the league.

> So we get into Cuba and we trained there. Oh it was hot. And we trained there very hard for two weeks and this was before Castro. I can remember one day they told us to bring sandwiches into the hotel because we were not going to practice or go out the next day because the army was walking down the streets. I can remember it was scary. Anyway the Brooklyn Dodgers were training there at the same time we were and we outdrew them. They came over and they said "What is going on over here?" and when they saw how well we played they couldn't believe it. Dottie Kamenshek was the first baseman for Rockford Peaches. They said if she had been a man they would have offered her $50,000 on the spot. In those days that was a lot, but that was a fun time.[37]

In Terry's retelling of the Cuban experience, the sight of soldiers walking through the streets barely gets a mention, but the fact that they had more fans than the men is a source of pride and clearly Terry's focus. It was not just being in Cuba that was significant but also playing ball there, in a country where baseball mattered in a different way, and where female players were treated with startling levels of respect and acceptance.

The other side of the coin was that the greater attention the women received could be uncomfortable. Helen Filarski was matter-of-fact about the challenges she faced while playing baseball in Cuba, but it is easy to see just how hard it was for her.

> In some ways it [playing in Cuba] was just another ball game. [But] it's another country and they start talking and I say, "ya, ya, sure," you don't know what they're talking about and they touch you. We were walking in a parade coming to the stadium one time and they touch you and get on the floor and holler, they just go out of their minds. They toss somebody and the guys that are keeping the line straight and they go up to them and are beating them with a Billy club and they didn't care how they hit them ... the police would get them if they would stick in their hand to touch you.

For a young girl from the Midwest, the invasion of personal space that Cuban fans displayed in trying to touch the players was disturbing. The experience of playing in Cuba was obviously a hard one for Helen, but later, when asked about what receiving those opportunities meant to her, she said, "It was something. When I think about it now I can't believe I was there and I think, look what I got to do."[38]

The lessons women drew from political and cultural differences, along with the excitement of playing ball outside the United States, would only continue on the Latin American tour. The tour provided life-changing experiences for the players, even those from Cuba. When Lefty Alvarez agreed to play baseball with the AAGPBL and the Cuban team on a South American exhibition tour, she had no idea how her life would change as a result of that experience. Both AAGPBL and Cuban players traveled to Guatemala City on January 26, where they spent four days. Of this experience Lefty said, "I just had to get on the plane. I don't know if my mother was sad or happy. She told me to go, so I did." There is no doubt that Lefty was scared that day. She remembered her fear when plane took off: "I had never done that before you know, take a plane. Wow, what was I getting into?" It was a bit easier for Lefty to settle into the game during this exhibition tour, as she had many other Spanish-speaking players to help her, especially since she spoke very little English. "I had such a hard time with the language," she said, "I could not understand unless they talked about baseball; then I could make some sense of it." She does not have a lot of memories of that tour, but the ones she does have focus on travel and experiencing life outside Cuba.[39]

From Guatemala the teams traveled to Managua, Nicaragua, where they stayed for nine days. While there the players were guests of Nicaraguan president Anastasio Somoza Garcia. This, according to Lefty, was a memory she will never forget: "Baseball in Nicaragua. With him, with Somoza. Hum. I did not know they like it so much."[40] Despite his brutal history as the president and dictator of Nicaragua, Somoza, like many other Nicaraguans, was a huge baseball fan. "In Nicaragua, baseball is and long has been '*el deporte rey*,' the king of sports."[41]

It was in this context that on February 1, 1949, the AAGPBL and Cuban players, including Lefty, visited the palace of President Somoza. One of the American players, Tiby Eisen, said,

> We were invited to the president's castle for an evening of feast, dance and entertainment. We all attended and the president was having such a good time that no one was allowed to leave. Our managers, Johnny Rawlings and Max Carey wanted us to leave but we were not allowed. This was one time we broke curfew and could not be fined. We all laugh about this. We danced all night— the rumba and other Latin American dances. [A g]ood time was had by all except our managers![42]

This account confirms Lefty's memory of the event. "He [the President] was charming," Lefty recalled.

> We all had to dress up. There was very good food and dance. Some of them danced, but I did not want to. But then General Somoza asked me to dance and I had to do it. He asked if I wanted to stay in Nicaragua with him. I said no. I was so scared but I do not think he meant it.[43]

Perhaps he did. Upon leaving the palace, Somoza's son took the hand of Annabelle Lee Harmon and said, "If there is anything I can do *to* you, let me know."[44]

Not only did Somoza host the players, but he also threw out the first pitch to begin the game between "los equipos cubano y norteam-ericano." His picture appeared on the front page of the local newspaper. The caption read, "General Anastasio Somoza, Minister of Defense, threw the first ball in the game between the Cuban and North American teams day before yesterday afternoon."[45]

For many of the American players, this event was the most impor-tant part of the tour. Being part of world events and meeting powerful people was exciting and transformative. But not so for Lefty. Instead, "making those first American friends" was the best thing, along with "seeing the Panama Canal. I did not care about that dictator. Maybe I feel different now that I am older, but I did not care about him then."[46] Only 15 years old, Lefty had little interest in politics and was not impressed by the opulence of the palace. All that mattered was the fact that she was playing baseball with her new American friends. Ironically, Lefty's first step toward becoming an American citizen was taken on the ball fields of Latin America.

Lefty Alvarez was afraid to fly. And, except for the train travel that got the players from place to place within countries, most of the inter-national tour traveling was done via airplanes. These were small planes, and many of the players reported being nervous as they boarded them for each trip. However, despite their fear, most remember the sights. Lefty said, "We flew over beautiful mountains, rivers through clouds, and I will never forget how the world looked from up there. I was scared most of the time—oh, the sights. Some of the girls rode in the cockpit, but not me. I was not that brave."[47]

Lefty's memory of that flight perfectly encapsulates what the expe-rience of travel meant to the AAGPBL players: the fear, the camaraderie, the adventure, the excitement of being challenged in new ways. Many of the women who played in the All-American Girls Professional Base-ball League point to these special memories of travel as the league's greatest gift to them. Most would agree that "seeing the world" was not among their main reasons for playing baseball, but now, some 70 years after the league's end, it is what they want to talk about, not their statistics (although most can recite those too).

It is true that exposure to new things, different people, and chal-lenging situations can make us stronger and help us to become more compassionate, open-minded individuals. Experiencing other cultures, both in and out of the United States, gave many of the former players of the AAGPBL the ability to grow in unanticipated ways. They used those lessons—to be more open to difference, to be more tolerant and to accept people more readily—throughout their lives after their playing time ended. Fortunately, this strength and compassion remains part of their legacy, there for current and future young women to see, experience, and use as a stepping-stone.

3

Patriotism
and Military Service

"Baseball is part of the American way of life. Remove it and you remove something from the lives of American citizens, soldiers and sailors."
—Private John E Stevenson, Fort Dix, New Jersey[1]

In 2011, the AAGPBL reunion was held in San Diego, California. And while a show of patriotism has been an important part of every reunion, this one was special. Docked in San Diego's harbor, the USS *Midway* was the site of one of the largest events ever held for the players. For some of the women, this allowed them to reconnect with the part of their league experience of which they are most proud: their service to the country. Upon arrival at the *Midway*, the players were met by men who served during World War II, veterans who volunteered on the ship. The women were first shown around the ship; then they were led to a line of tables set up in the enormous open-air hanger. It had been advertised that the players would be present on the *Midway* for an autograph session and a screening of the movie *A League of Their Own*, and a small crowd was expected. Once the women were seated and ready to receive the crowd, I walked to the edge of the ship and looked over the side. I could not believe the length of the line of people waiting to get on the ship. A steady stream of fans kept the women signing autographs much longer than the hour allotted for this part of the event. And once the film began, the huge crowd, estimated at nearly 650, sat down alongside the players to watch the movie that changed their lives. It is always special when the players get to meet fans and talk to them about the league, but to do it on that ship, a symbol of America's determination and courage during the war, strengthened the patriotic thread that tied the league to America's wartime experience.

In nearly every interview with former players who played during and immediately after World War II, the women talk about their role in making life in America better during wartime. They point to the ways in which the league helped the war effort by displaying patriotism, entertaining troops, visiting Red Cross hospitals and, as Earlene "Beans" Risinger (1948–1954) said, "keeping America's pastime healthy."[2] Decades after the war's end, members of the AAGPBL remain extremely proud of their wartime service to the United States. Strikingly, historians tend to see the legacy of the AAGPBL almost exclusively in terms of its impact on the history of sports and women's history. The fact that the league was founded during wartime is seen as important primarily because the demands of the war created a new space for women's professional sports. The players themselves, however, see the situation the other way around. Many would agree with Beans that the role they played in "helping to win World War II" was the most significant aspect of their time in the league. "We were patriots," Beans explained, and playing professional baseball was an expression of that patriotism.[3] While today the former players recognize their many contributions to women's history and women's sports, for them the AAGPBL was a piece of World War II history, first and foremost.

In some ways this is not surprising. After all, the league originated in Wrigley's desire to support the war effort. When FDR wrote the "Green Light Letter" calling for baseball to endure, he was thinking about how game maintained morale at home. It is possible that Philip Wrigley created the All-American Girls Professional Baseball League (initially the All-American Girls Softball League) as a way to support the war effort. He certainly did a lot of work on the home front: He contributed to programs designed to boost the war effort, including dismantling the large electric sign on Times Square long before Broadway dimmed its lights for the blackout. He donated the flood lights that lit the Wrigley building to the U.S. Navy and voluntarily surrendered the company's entire 5,000,000-pound inventory of aluminum ingots reserved for wrapping foil. He donated his advertisement time on the radio to help sell war bonds. And he closed his tourist business

At every reunion there is an attempt to get a group photograph of the players present. It is never easy, as this photograph from San Diego illustrates. Once the photographs are taken the players always begin singing their song. "Batter Up" (photograph by Cami J. Kidder).

on Catalina Island so that the U.S. government could use it for training. Wrigley, like other manufacturers, also converted part of his gum factory to an assembly line for packing K rations. Arguably, he was dedicated to helping the American war effort, but he was also a businessman with a connection to sports. Both factors likely came together in his creation of the AAGPBL.[4]

Support for the military and the home front was built into the league's work in ways that made it inescapable for players. AAGPBL officials demanded that the league always display patriotism. This took on many forms. At the beginning of each game, the two teams came together to form a "V" for Victory that stretched from home plate down the first and third baselines; then they stood at attention while a band played the national anthem. The women also played exhibition games

Jacqueline "Jackie" Baumgart (left; former player) and associate member Debbie Pierson. Jackie was a strong advocate for girls in sports, and she hosted numerous AAGPBL reunions. She also convinced Billie Jean King to attend the final reunion she organized, in Milwaukee. Jackie passed away just as this book was being completed (photograph by Cami J. Kidder).

to support the Red Cross and the armed forces, and visited wounded veterans at army hospitals.[5]

Many of the players remember that, at the time, they just played the game and did not think about making history of any kind on the baseball diamond. They always understood, however, that they were providing an important service during the war. As Jacqueline Baumgart (1950–1951) explained,

> We were very much aware of sort of a role, I would call it a role, that a—that actually helped to keep people who worked very hard and long hours, they had a chance to relax and had a chance to interact with us, and we with them, in a very positive way. We were always in tune with what was going on, always. We began every game with the "Star Spangled Banner" and we were very in tune to "God Bless America." We sang all the time and it was the singing that helped us in the sense of fulfilling what it is that the people at home had to go through

and keep the moral[e]—we were moral[e] boosters, I would say for whomever came in contact with us.[6]

Some players saw that role as the whole point of the league. As Joyce McCoy (1943) explained, "I thought [at the time] our purpose was to entertain the troops and the defense workers, that's my idea."[7] It was also the idea of Arthur Meyerhoff, the league's advertising executive. One of his first publicity themes was "Recreation for War Workers," which furthered Wrigley's aim of supporting both baseball and the war effort. Many of the cities that hosted the first league teams were chosen because they were also near large industrial plants.[8] Manufacturing plants in areas like Kenosha, Wisconsin, and South Bend, Indiana, had converted their plants to war production, and Meyerhoff believed that there was a particular need to provide those workers with affordable entertainment. Teams often set aside special nights at the ball park for workers, and advertisements made the connection to wartime morale explicit. As one ad for a Kenosha Comets game proclaimed,

> Come out and have the time of your life! ... They're the top players of the country, keenly competing, upholding the best traditions of big-league play, boosting morale and providing the finest recreation on our home front![9]

The league even played day games on occasion so that workers from the second shift could attend.

Thus, while many players admit they did not think about it at the time, they later realized that what they were doing really was part of the war effort, at least in the sense of building morale and entertaining Americans during a stressful time. But this isn't enough to explain why so many of them see their patriotic work as their most important legacy. To understand that, it helps to look at the broader meaning of patriotism and the larger context of the AAGPBL players' lives.

For the former players, patriotism wasn't just defined by a set of acts they accomplished; it saturated their whole league experience. As Joyce McCoy remembered, "I think we felt, I did anyway, more patriotic at that time, so when we went out on the field, the first thing we did was march out in a V for victory for the armed forces."[10] Although the league in fact required women to create that V, for McCoy this act was an authentic expression of her feelings at the time.

Baseball itself was central to that expression of patriotic sentiment.

3. *Patriotism and Military Service*

While "playing baseball during war time may seem unimportant to some," as Beans pointed out, "to us, well, we really believed that we were helping to keep an important part of American culture alive." As Beans explained it, during World War II,

> Everything, anything that said "America" was worth saving. We knew the boys needed to know that life back home was the same and that what they were fighting for would be here when they got back. They left it up to us and we came through.[11]

Everything American was worth saving, and baseball represents American culture like no other sport. Baseball is part of the fabric of America. It is played on diamonds, in fields and on the streets of every town and city. Former player Karen Kunkel (1952) put this idea especially well:

> We [Americans] needed continuity in our country, and our soldiers needed to know that when they returned from war some things—like baseball, apple pie, and the all-American girl—would still be here for them.[12]

Many players have expressed versions of this determination to do their part, and their belief that they succeeded is part of why they believe patriotism remains their most important legacy.

The meaning of patriotism goes even deeper for some players. They emphasize the importance of the league's wartime work by equating their time playing baseball with military service. Jacqueline Baumgart is a perfect example. While she played after the war ended, the memories of the war years and the sense that the league was an important part of the effort to win the war made her proud of what she called her "service to the effort."

> You know, we grew up in a time when we were at WWII and my husband was in WWII, I had two of my brothers in WWII and we took care of the home front in the sense of—when we played we made a V from home plate past the pitcher's mound, one team here and one team there and that V was for victory, that's what that was for. We played at Fort Sheridan for the soldiers there and for the navy people at Great Lakes and that was usually in the springtime for exhibitions and things like that. We helped to sell war bonds in the sense of our appearances. We didn't physically handle that, but it was because of whom we were and what we were doing that the war bonds were sold and we saved Aluminum foil and made it into baseballs and threw them around. We were a part of the home front; I think a very large part of the home front. To give

entertainment where there wasn't much. You didn't have much money, there was gas rationing and we took care of the people in that sense that were in a geographical area.[13]

Jacqueline's linking of her male relatives' military service to the work of the league, and her emphasis on how the league "took care of the people" the way the military "takes care" of the defense of the country, powerfully ties the league to the larger military effort during the war.

For many of the AAGPBL players, playing professional baseball was only one part of a lifetime of service to the country. Women who recognize strong links between their various patriotic commitments often make the stronger claims for the importance of that part of the league's legacy. In fact, many of the players participated in the war industry while playing ball. Jerre DeNoble (1947) worked at a company called Glass House in California making "those big floats for the Submarines and stuff like that." Well known to the community as a good ball player, Jerre was first hired by the company to play on the Glass House softball team. Later, she convinced them to hire her as a bottle inspector. Despite the long hours, she was glad to do her part for the war effort: "[Between] working sixteen-hour shift[s] in the Glass House ... and playing ball ... we didn't get much rest.... Three or four hours sleep a day.... I didn't mind though. I was doing my part."[14] When she wasn't working in the factory or playing ball, DeNoble coached the team fielded by the Navy Women's Reserve unit called the Women Accepted for Volunteer Emergency Service (WAVES). She did not play with the WAVES, as they were stationed in Hawaii, but she did help them practice when they were in California. "They were stationed in for a month or whatever because they were stationed in Hawaii and all different places, so it was hard to travel with them. But I did coach them while they were here."

Despite her busy life, working and coaching softball, Jerre was convinced by a friend to try out for the AAGPBL.

Well, I didn't know a thing about it, but Dottie—Dorothy Stolze, I called her Dottie, I grew up with her. She lived about three houses up from me and we played softball on the same team. How she found out, I don't know, but she approached me one day and said, "Jerre, they're going to have tryouts in San Francisco and they're going to send a scout out. Let's go over and tryout for baseball," and I said, "I don't know if I want to." I had a job and I had a lot of years and built up seniority that I didn't want to lose, but she said, "Let's give it a try," so I did, I went over with her and there were like five hundred gals that were there. They hit balls to us and grounders and fly balls over our shoulder and did about everything they could do, but have us stand on our heads. They didn't say nothing to us and about two weeks, I guess, later I got a letter from Max Carey stating to go get a Passport and my birth certificate, and that we would be receiving a ticket for a flight, to Havana, Cuba. That's how we found out we were going to play ball.... I was hesitant, but once—if fact I didn't really want to go and my supervisor he told me, "Jerre," he said, "We'll give you a leave of absence, you won't lose any time on the job, we'll stop your time and then when you come back we'll start it again ... it's a chance of a lifetime you'll probably never ever get again," so I went.

Jerre's playing career lasted for only the 1947 season. She suffered a broken ankle while teaching the WAVES how to hook slide. The injury was so severe that it ended her playing days. She went back to Glass House, where she worked for forty years. In her view, all of these activities were linked. Whether it was working in the factory, coaching the WAVES, or playing baseball with the AAGPBL, Jerre believed that she was a "part of the war effort on every level." Perhaps that recognition helps explain her belief that "we were, are patriotic, it was the best thing we did."

For some players, the connection between the league and military service was more immediate. Ball players from the AAGPBL served in every branch of service open to women during World War II. Some served during the war, some after, and others made the military their career. In every case, they are proud veterans, and they always tell their stories as if the two threads of their lives, their military and baseball histories, were intertwined.

There were four military options for women during World War II: the U.S. Army established the Women's Army Auxiliary Corps (WAAC),[15] the U.S. Navy recruited women into the WAVES, the Marine Corps formed the Marine Corps Women's Reserve, and the Coast Guard established a Women's Reserve known as the SPARs (after the motto *Semper Paratus*—"Always Ready"). In each of these branches of service, women served in a variety of jobs, including communications, medicine, administration, supply, photography and food service. The Women Airforce Service Pilots (WASPs), which, unlike the other groups, was not an auxiliary group of an existing military branch, consisted of experienced aviators.[16] All told, 350,000 American women served in the U.S. military during World War II, or about one out of every 200 women. Sixteen were killed in action.[17]

Twenty-three women from the AAGPBL served in the U.S. military either before or after their time in the league.[18] This was one out of twenty-six players, a much higher percentage than in the general population. This ratio suggests that patriotism and service were especially important for women who played baseball. Three former members of the AAGPBL—Helen Campbell (1947–1949), Helen "Gig" Smith (1947–1948), and Elma "Steck" Weiss (1948–1949)—have stories that illuminate the connections between the military and the league in lives shaped by service to the nation.

Initially, Gig Smith, who grew up in Richmond, Virginia, thought the idea of playing professional baseball was a distraction from the larger call to service, even before the bombing of Pearl Harbor. When Gig was first offered a tryout for the AAGPBL, she declined. She told them, "I'm going into the service. Because everybody was doing something—it was a different war—everybody was collecting things, scrap metal, everybody was doing something, and I wanted to go in too."[19] After listening to news of the Japanese attack on Pearl Harbor, Gig "went back to the kitchen where my mother was, and I said ... I wished that they had something for women to do. I'd love to go in." She watched her brothers and other male friends and family members join the military, but Gig had to wait until the women's auxiliaries were created, which began in 1942. Finally, she headed to the Marine recruiting station.

The fellow at the recruiting station was very rude—he kept his head down and wrote—and I stood there waiting. It seems like a half hour but it couldn't have been more than a few minutes. Then he said, "what do you want?" And that threw me back. And I said, what do you mean what do I want? I'd like to know a little bit about the Marines. He said—still writing and still not looking up—what do you want to know about the Marines? ... I don't remember what was said after that, and I could hardly wait to get out of there, and I walked down those steps and down about 8 blocks to the Army recruiting station. The fellow was totally different. He was opposite of the rough old marine that didn't look immaculate in his dress, and this was a young black fellow that stood up and introduced himself and put his hand out when he introduced himself, and he said—What can I help you with? And I said—I'd like to know a little bit about the Army. And he said—Have a seat and we'll see what we can do.

Needless to say, Gig joined the army. Because of her interest in and talent for art, she worked in publications until she was transferred to the Pentagon. There, she worked in a wartime department that decoded Japanese messages.

> We had people on islands that the Japanese didn't know about, and if the Japanese had known about them, they would have of course beheaded them. But they intercepted their codes as the ships went by. They sent them to our department. Now, I did not do the decoding, but it was within our department. It was all secret. Everything that they sent us—little pieces of paper with information on it, where the ships were, what they were carrying, what the weight of the ship was—they sent to us to plot on these maps, and we determined which ones would be bombed, which would help to shorten the war. Actually, we were as close to the war as you could get for not being there. It was fascinating.

After the war ended, Gig had an opportunity to go to Japan with the occupational forces, but she also wanted to attend college. Ultimately, she decided to attend art school in New York but found it difficult.

> I went to Pratt until ... I was trying to live on 79 dollars a month, and it was pretty rough, so I called the [AAGPBL] scout that had offered me the contract that I had turned down to go into the service, to see if I could still get that contract. And that weekend, they had me flying from New York to Chicago.

After meeting with AAGPBL administrators, Gig flew to Kenosha, where she played for the remainder of that season, continuing her education during the off-season. Her only full season in the AAGPBL was the following year, 1948, which she spent in Grand Rapids.

Gig played in the league until a family crisis intervened.

> My mother was sick and my father wrote me a very sweet letter, asking me to consider if I would come home to help him. So I had to transfer from Pratt to what's now VCU [Virginia Commonwealth University], and I had to stop playing softball, too, and baseball.

Gig went back to Richmond, Virginia, where she helped to care for her family. After finishing her degree at Virginia Commonwealth University, she taught in the Richmond public school system for 31 years. Despite having originally seen baseball as a "distraction," Gig came to understand that it was as much a patriotic endeavor as her military career. As she put it, "In both cases, I served my country."

No one represents the dual war effort better than Helen Hannah Campbell, Marine and AAGPBL chaperone. Helen was a career Marine whose dedication to the military was represented by the high rank she achieved—that of master gunnery sergeant. Strikingly, even someone so committed to the military remembers her baseball experience as part of a continuum of patriotic service.

Born in Salt Lake City, Utah, Helen earned a degree in business administration and a secondary journalism degree at Woodbury College. But when the war broke out, she took a job in a defense plant. When she found there was no opportunity for promotion, she decided to join the Marine Corps. Her experience was quite different from Gig Smith's:

> The Marines were the last to take women because the commandant didn't want skirts with his male Marines. But we showed 'em. For the ladies that followed, they have so much more than we had. They have 225 [job] possibilities [today] and we only had 30. Back then, you couldn't be married or pregnant. Now they have child care centers all over the place and encourage married women and men to stay on the base. Now that I look back on it, we went down the path first and opened up a lot of doors to the young women that came behind us. The overall scope of my work was administration and paperwork.... Those years were fun. It was disastrous because you knew what was happening to the boys, but it was a good job. It was a good career and I've never regretted a minute of it.[20]

After retiring from active duty in 1946, Helen joined the Marine Corps Reserves. That was when she got "tangled up in baseball."[21]

Baseball ran in Helen's family: "My father was a professional baseball player for 30 years. They called him 'Truck' Hannah because he was big and slow. He played for the Yankees after World War I and played with Babe Ruth."[22] Helen went with her father to the 1946 annual meeting of major league baseball, and there she met Max Carey, president of the AAGPBL. Knowing that Helen was just out of the Marines, Carey asked about her job situation, promising to call her about an opportunity with the AAGPBL. In the spring of 1947, Carey offered Helen a job: "Within a very short time I found myself in Chicago getting ready to go to spring training in Cuba.... I became the chaperone for the Muskegon Lassies of Michigan."[23] Helen served as the Lassies' chaperone from 1947 to 1950. In 1950, the team moved to Kalamazoo, and Helen moved with them. She described her job as one that kept her busy all day, every day, and one that she loved.

> They were a good bunch of ball players. They were athletes. We [the chaperones] became surrogate mothers to them. You arranged their housing, uniforms, got their paychecks, arranged the buses. But they really accepted me more like a buddy. If they wanted to go out and get a burger and a beer, I'd go with them.[24]

Helen stayed with the Kalamazoo team until 1951, when she was recalled to active duty with the start of the Korean War. After the war, she made the Marine Corps her career. Helen retired in 1975, after thirty-two years in service. Yet even in retirement, Helen's life centered around patriotism and service to the United States. Having been to high school with Richard M. Nixon, she remained a supporter of the president throughout her life. So it was natural for her to become a docent at the Richard Nixon Library.

Years after her Marine Corps and AAGPBL careers ended, Helen remained proud of both. And she recalled each experience in similar terms:

> I am a patriot. Proud to do my part and proud I had three chances to do so. One in World War II, one with the AAGPBL, and one during the Korean War. I loved every minute of it. Semper Fi.[25]

Being patriotic, doing her part for the country, also meant everything to Elma "Steck" Weiss (1948–1949). Steck (her maiden name, but also a nickname used by almost all of the ball players when referring to Elma) grew up in Columbus, Ohio, and attended Ohio State University. Determined to do something that mattered, something that would have an impact on the world, she was confronted with a choice:

> I completed three years and then the war changed people's lives dramatically, as you know, and we had we had a shortage of teachers, but the rule at that time was, if you had completed three years of college and you could get a principal to hire you, you could teach school, so that's what I did. After my third year I went to Port Clinton, Ohio, and taught high school for a year.

The experience of doing something for others had a powerful impact on Steck. After her year was up, she was expected to return to school.

But there remained "the urge, the desire to be patriotic again—instead of finishing my senior year I joined the navy."[26]

After enlisting, Steck immediately headed to New York for "six weeks of basic training." The WAVES were all expected to pick an area of emphasis in their studies, and she chose "physical education, so I had another three months in New York City." The physical aspects of basic training were very different for the women, although both men and women were expected to abide by codes of discipline. As Steck remembered,

> For the WAVES they tried to get us familiar with navy terms and so forth, and we had to learn that the floor was the deck and the stairs were ladders and so forth, so we spoke in navy terms and we were taught to recognize and identify airplanes and ships and so forth. Just so we could—we didn't expect to get aboard a ship, and of course we didn't, but we knew all the navy lingo and that's the way they wanted it. It was not as physical as it was for the men. But, we were under the same rules. I went home for Christmas at one time and we were snowed in on the train coming back and in the navy they don't care about a snowstorm. What happens if you miss your ship? The war might hinge on you making your ship, so [if we were late to report] we had to serve what they call "a captain's mast" and you had to work cleaning the decks or something of that nature. They treated us like the young men in that way.

For Steck, the punishment wasn't necessarily a bad thing; she learned from it and saw the importance of the lesson about responsibility.

Steck spent two years in the navy, doing a number of jobs ranging from teaching to running a recreational room for naval personnel. Her favorite memory, and perhaps her proudest moment, was of an event that happened by accident:

> I use to play a trumpet years ago and I recall one time we were raising the flag on our post and several officers came out and I practiced raising the reveille in the morning and [I] took some pictures of that and that was kind of thrilling and exciting too. It was kind of exciting with all the people standing around saluting and watching the flag go up.

Steck was discharged from the navy in 1945. She continued her education after her discharge, and it was while she was working on her master's degree in Berkeley, California, in 1948 that Steck was first introduced to the AAGPBL. She played softball with some of the local women, and one of them encouraged her to contact Bill Allington, a scout for the league at that time. She made the cut, and, as she said, "the next thing I knew I was in Peoria, Illinois. I was sent there to play with the Red Wings."

Making an impact on the world was important to Steck, and whether the discussion is about her military career, her teaching career, or her time playing baseball, she was very accomplished. But she is especially proud of what she accomplished on the field as a girl.

> Of all the things I've done, the college degrees and the teaching and getting married and having children and all of that, I recall that the baseball was the thing that I remember the most and enjoyed the most of all the things I've done in my life. In eighty-seven years you do a lot of living. But I think the baseball stands out because, we played softball on the playground and I just knew since I was a kid—I remember I use to play in the second grade, at recess we would play and at a high school reunion one time a man said to me, "when you were in the second grade everyone wanted you on their team," because not too many girls played, just the boys, and they knew that I could play some, so they enjoyed that and I enjoyed that also. I just always played.

Steck valued the sense that she was part of something much larger than herself. You can see this in her description of the crowds that the AAGPBL drew:

> The crowds were so large. The biggest crowd I ever played before in the baseball was ten thousand. Everybody would stand outside the locker room and wait for the girls to shower and then they would sign autographs and you begin to think you have some importance in this world.

First as a member of the U.S. Navy, then as a professional baseball player, Elma "Steck" Weiss did make a difference in the world. Her drive to contribute, along with her sense of patriotism and duty, led her to join the navy and pushed her to earn a graduate degree (and eventually a PhD). In addition, it shaped her sense that the most important legacy of the league was the larger service it provided to the nation.

There is little doubt that the AAGPBL and its players helped America cope with the challenges of wartime. That success remains for the players a critical example of why the league should be remembered as an important part of World War II history. Their home-front role is what they turn to when explaining why playing baseball was patriotic. But patriotism took on many different manifestations for the women of the AAGPBL. Some players believed that their time in the league, entertaining war production workers and troops who were stateside, was their patriotic duty. Others worked in the war industry, and some players served in the military during and after World War II. No matter how they served, all would agree that helping the country win the war, both on and off the battlefield, was one of their most significant contributions.

Although the players talk about their war role as an important part of their legacy, they also demonstrate their awareness of the impact they have had on girls and women. They might not identify as feminist heroes, but many certainly see them in that way. Whether it was Gig's run-in with the Marine recruiter, Helen's pride in the level of rank and leadership she achieved as a Marine, or Steck's experience of being the only girl chosen for a sports team, these women serve for generations of girls who came after them as a shining example of what strong women can achieve.

4

A Revolution in Sports

"Finally someone noticed. Boy, did they notice."—Lefty Alvarez[1]

It has been a number of years since my students' challenge to find examples of women who gained substantial benefits from playing sports led me to the players' reunion of the All-American Girls Professional Baseball League. In every women's history class since that one, I have replayed the discussion about Title IX, the federal law that requires equal access to sports and other activities in institutions that receive federal funds. I still have students who question the necessity and importance of Title IX and whether women still need that protection. Former league players recognize that perhaps their greatest legacy is the bridge they provide between an era when women were expected to remain sedentary and the competitive, high-quality play of female athletes today. Women of the AAGPBL are proud of what they accomplished as ball players, and also of how they helped society see what women could do on the playing field if given a chance. At each year's reunion, the players invite local softball teams to join them in watching the movie that made the league popular: *A League of Their Own.* Afterward, the players sit for hours while young girls file past with various objects to be autographed: gloves, balls, shirts, and even socks. The players talk to each person and, after literally hours, emerge– "stiff but happy!"

While at a recent reunion, I asked a group of players how they could sit and sign autographs for that long. One of them asked, "Have you ever heard of Title IX?" I assured her that I had. And then, with a great deal of passion, each and every one of them talked to me about how we must, at all costs, protect what they believe they helped to

81

start, and what Title IX represents: a revolution in women's sports. As the next group of young girls approached the autograph table, I backed away. I couldn't help but feel jealous as they, the first generation of girls who could dream with certainty of an athletic future, bombarded the players with questions about playing professional baseball.

From 1943 to 1954, numerous young women were given the chance of a lifetime—the opportunity to earn a good salary by playing professional baseball. As a result, they inadvertently created the foundation on which a "revolution in women's sports" would develop. Their ground-breaking effort began on the playing field and continued for decades as they became teachers, role models, and advocates for women and girls in sports. The former players challenged the limits of who and what girls could be through exceeding gender expectations in their own lives. Whether they served as the first female athletic director of a major university, as a director of an Olympic training center, as teachers, coaches or personal role models, the women who played in the All-American Girls Professional Baseball League were living, breathing examples of what access to sports could do for girls and women. It was their decades-long example that bridged the gap between the end of the AAGPBL and Title IX, the explosion of opportunities for girls and women in sports.

Title IX, which requires that girls be granted equal access to sports and other activities, was critical to that revolution. Since its passage in 1972, Title IX has opened doors for millions of women and girls to take part in competitive athletics. While fewer than 32,000 women participated in college sports prior to the enactment of Title IX, today that number has expanded nearly five-fold, or more than 400 percent—to approximately 163,000 women.[2] Opportunities for girls at the high school level have grown dramatically as well. Female participation in high school athletics has increased each year and set an all-time high of 3,267,664 between 2012 and 2013.[3]

This revolution is one of the most significant changes for girls and women in American history. For many, including some of my students, sports are frivolous, unimportant activities. However, sports help women realize that integrity, creativity, passion, and hard work are important elements of success, and that true victory is defined long after the game is over. Sports are where men have traditionally learned about teamwork, goal setting, the pursuit of excellence, and other achievement-oriented behaviors; now these benefits are available to women as well. Like their male counterparts, women who play sports are more successful in business and more likely than other women to become leaders. In fact, a study by OppenheimerFunds found that four out of five executive businesswomen (82 percent) played sports growing up, and the vast majority say that the lessons they learned on the playing field have contributed to their success.[4]

There is no doubt that women and girls who participate in sports are healthier than those who do not, and there are hundreds of reports pointing to the fact that taking part in sports increases young women's self-esteem. Sports also provide academic benefits. According to a study conducted by the Feminist Majority Foundation at the turn of the twentieth century, high school students (both girls and boys) who participated in sports had higher grades than non-athletes, and a larger percentage of athletes scored in the top percentile on standardized tests.[5] Both rural and urban youths who played sports had lower drop-out rates, and athletes were more likely than non-athletes to describe themselves in favorable terms.[6] The benefits of sports are numerous and show up both in and out of the classroom. This revolution matters to American girls because sports matter, and the women of the AAGPBL are very proud of having helped to start that movement.

Many AAGPBL players believe they were a direct part of the revolution in women's sports though their impact on Title IX. "We helped build the bridge to Title IX," explained Audrey Daniels.

> We showed that we were as equal as boys. Coming into sports and giving the women's sports the same consideration that you're giving the boys and we did you know, chapter nine [Title IX] was passed for equal opportunity in sports and I think we accomplished a great deal and we're proud of what we did, we're very proud of it.[7]

Players are careful to recognize the importance of other female athletes, including Billie Jean King, who were part of the transformation of women in sports. But this does not take away from the critical role that the women of the AAGPBL played in challenging gender roles, acting as role models, and teaching and coaching younger generations of girls.

The athletic ability of the women in the AAGPBL challenged and ultimately made a mockery of the socially constructed feminine roles of the mid-twentieth century. Women in the AAGPBL did not abide by the accepted gender ideology of the time. Rather, they engaged in behavior—playing baseball—that seemed appropriate to them, even though society had defined sports as traditionally masculine. Their success created a new model of athletic femininity that expanded the vision of opportunity for girls interested in sports. Power, strength, and determination were shown to be female attributes, too. The AAGPBL offered the public an expanded view of female capabilities and demonstrated that athleticism and femininity need not be mutually exclusive.

Changing the public image of women was crucial to creating the groundwork for the revolution. The traditional 1950s image of women wearing makeup and pearls to do housework was challenged by the dirty-faced, hard-nosed baseball players of the AAGPBL. Both images appeared on the covers of popular magazines. Although AAGPBL players were expected to maintain a feminine image (and they did), they also transcended that image. Their fierceness, determination and strength shone through the skirts and the makeup, igniting a feminist challenge to society's conservative images of women.

It wasn't just through their AAGPBL image that the players had an impact, however. Almost all of them continued to play sports after the league ended. For some it was recreational softball; for others it was tennis, volleyball, golf, bowling or fishing. The type of sports and the level of competition changed as they aged, but the desire to compete never waned. And an astonishing number went on to be coaches and teachers.[8] Through working with children, they could pass on their love of sports, as well as the lessons they learned while playing. Former player Earlene Beans Risinger (1948–1954) agreed:

> We want girls to know that they can also benefit from time playing sports. Not everyone will have the chance we did and they may not ever get paid for playing, but it teaches them to be strong and to think for themselves.... That may be our most important legacy, that message, girls can be strong, should be strong.

Years after she played her last game, Beans had not lost the self-confidence she developed while playing for the Grand Rapids Chicks, nor had she forgotten the key lesson she learned, one that she always shared with young people: "Shoot for the moon, and if you fail or fall, you will still be among the stars.... I wanted all those kids to know the joy of sports, of baseball. It can change your life."[9] That lifelong connection to sports and the need to share the joy of athletics with younger generations was present in the reminiscences of most of the former players.

Beans also saw a direct connection between what she did as a coach and the increased opportunities for girls:

> We feel that we helped women get to play more sports. When I first came to Grand Rapids and stayed in the wintertime, I said, "What do the girls get to do in high school and around?" Well, they didn't get to do anything and I feel now that ... we were stepping stones for the younger generation.... We feel like we made our mark in that respect.[10]

After the passage of Title IX, the opportunities in women's athletics were even greater. Teams, schools, and organizations sought experienced female athletes to coach, manage and organize programs for women. Former players of the AAGPBL were the perfect candidates. Mary Pratt (1943–1947) demonstrated this link: "With the advent of Title IX, in the 1970s, competition in girls' athletic programs increased, and I became very active in the local and state associations, serving in leadership roles, at every level."[11] The AAGPBL players' experiences and ongoing advocacy for women's sports laid the groundwork for many of the current sports opportunities enjoyed by women today. They relished the opportunities they had and did their part to make future positions available to women.

In all of these ways—defying gender expectations, playing ball, coaching and advocating for female athletes—the players were part of the revolution in women's sports. But for many former players, the fact that they became role models for girls, showing them what determination and hard work can do, is what they find most satisfying. "Our images, the fact that we played when we did and as hard as we did, showed the country what women can do on the ball field," Beans explained. "But more important than that, it showed young girls what *they* could do."[12]

The role modeling offered by players from the AAGPBL extended beyond athletics. The educational and professional success of the players later in life demonstrated how the traits of confidence, independence, and autonomy that were developed and refined on the playing field could also benefit young girls in academic and professional pursuits. The careers of former players were varied, with some becoming doctors, lawyers, professors, teachers and principals. But all of these role models encouraged girls to follow their dreams.

Women of the AAGPBL showed a generation of young women not only that women can play sports but also that women can play them well and benefit greatly from having that experience. These players were living, breathing proof that, when given the chance, women can and do make a difference on the playing field and, as a result, can also make a huge difference off the field. The stories of Audrey Wagner, Maddy English, Katie Horstman, Jean Cione, and Karen Violetta Kunkel illustrate both the physical and the social importance of women's sports. In addition, they reflect on what many female athletes today say is perhaps the most important legacy of the AAGPBL: the presence of strong female role models. From the 1940s through the 1950s the AAGPBL players' images—strong, determined, athletic—graced the covers of national magazines. They showed the public, especially young girls, that women played baseball, and they played it at a high level. But those images transcended sports, Terry Donahue claimed. Pointing to the importance of seeing other strong, successful women and how that helps girls feel empowered, she said, "Seeing someone else do something first and succeed at it makes it easier for others to follow. That's how you start a revolution. That's what we did."[13]

Few of the former players represent personal and public success like Audrey Wagner (1943–1949). She was born and raised in Bensenville, Illinois, a small town near Chicago. Like so many of her teammates, Audrey began playing sandlot baseball with the boys in her neighborhood. When she turned fifteen, she heard about the AAGPBL, and in 1943 she became one of the sixty original members of the league and was assigned to the Kenosha Comets, where she spent her entire AAGPBL career. Audrey was a two-time member of the All-Star Team.

Despite the fact that Audrey was a talented baseball player and, according to her brother, was recognized as a natural athlete, realizing her dream of becoming a doctor was her first priority. Through both high school and college, Audrey insisted on finishing the school year before playing full time. In fact, she did not make the 1947 spring training

4. A Revolution in Sports

trip to Cuba because school was still in session. Audrey was not a woman of means, and she was aware of the cost of medical school. The money she earned as a player in the AAGPBL went a long way toward making her dream a reality. As her brother wrote in response to a National Baseball Hall of Fame survey,

> She worked as a pin setter for a bowling alley, a store clerk, and a newspaper delivery person to earn money in the off season.... Audrey did anything she could to make a dollar. After she finished playing, she took the money she earned and fulfilled her dream of becoming a doctor. The league gave her that chance.

When Audrey was on the playing field, however, she was as dedicated to baseball as she was to her studies. In 1947 Audrey had a .305 batting average and led the circuit in home runs, doubles, and total bases. She lost the batting crown by a single point to Dorothy Kamenshek (1943–1953) and was named to the All-Star Team. In 1948, she won the batting title, was named the Player of the Year and again made the All-Star Team.[14] As her statistics indicate, Audrey's career with the AAGPBL was very successful. In 1950, she moved to the National Girls Baseball League (NGBL), which actually played softball, because it was closer to school and paid higher salaries. While playing ball, Wagner attended Elmhurst College, where she received her bachelor's degree in pre-medicine. She then went to the University of Illinois for her medical degree, going on to become an obstetrician and gynecologist.

Audrey was accomplished in many aspects of her public life and visibly challenged gender limitations. She even earned her private pilot's license in the 1950s, which was very uncommon for a woman, and later she became a local political official, serving on the city council in Crescent City, California. In every one of these cases, Audrey stepped outside society's prescribed gender roles for women and provided a public example for other girls. According to her brother, she remained grateful for the "physical, financial and emotional" opportunities that playing professional baseball provided. Audrey died at the age of 56 while piloting a small plane in Wyoming.[15] In what was ultimately a short life, Audrey Wagner accomplished a great deal, and much of it was because she had access to sports. What she did with that experience and how she continued to use it to challenge gender norms made her an important role model.

The All-American Girls After the AAGPBL

The life of Madeline "Maddy" English (1943–1950) builds on the story of success and social change that Audrey represents. Maddy grew up playing multiple sports, often with her brothers and other boys in her neighborhood. Her favorite sport, however, was baseball. One of her brothers, Edward, was a star third baseman in high school, but unfortunately military service during World War II dashed any hopes he had of turning professional. As it turned out, Maddy was the only one of the English children to play professional baseball.

In 1943, a baseball scout who had seen her play softball at a summer exhibition game in 1939 invited Maddy to a tryout at Wrigley Field in Chicago, Illinois. With two siblings in the Marines, she was reluctant to leave her parents, but with the encouragement of her whole family, she attended the tryout. "I was in awe of everything," Maddy remembered. "I never saw so many girls playing baseball before. There must have been two hundred women trying out at Wrigley Field. They told us they only needed sixty players for four teams."[16] Maddy was assigned to the Racine Belles. She was one of the original players to sign with the league, and her team won the first AAGPBL Championship Title.

Before the 1951 season, when the team moved from Racine, Wisconsin, to Battle Creek, Michigan, Maddy and some of the other original Belles decided not to make the move. During the first eight years of their existence, the Belles were a close-knit team, like a family away from home. Maddy and her teammates thought that everything would change following the transition, so they decided to retire rather than move to Michigan. "For me the league was over," Maddy said. "After playing eight years with the same team, I did not want to change. So, I quit."[17] Although she retired from the AAGPBL, she did not retire from sports altogether. She continued to play recreational sports but also spent much of her life coaching, teaching and encouraging girls to be active.

Despite her successes on the field, Maddy understood that she needed to plan for her future after baseball. Even with her family's support, being a woman in the 1950s meant it would take every ounce of courage and willpower Maddy possessed to be successful. She was determined to get an education, but since she combined going to college with playing baseball, she was limited to the off-season, when she attended evening and Saturday classes at Boston University. After she retired from the AAGPBL, Maddy worked as a recreational leader in Everett. It took her nine years to graduate, but she finally earned her bachelor of science in education in 1957, and then a master's degree in 1962. The financial stability provided by her baseball career was crucial to her ability to stay in school. But it was more than that. As Maddy recalled, "The courage and sense of self-worth I gained from the baseball experience made everything seem possible."[18]

Long after her playing days were over, Maddy remained part of the revolution in women's sports. She continued to play softball and basketball, coached girls' softball, and took the time to serve as a spokesperson for the AAGPBL, accepting speaking engagements around the country. Through a twenty-seven-year career at Parlin Junior High School, she worked first as a classroom and physical education teacher, and then as the school's guidance counselor. Maddy mentored students in all three capacities, showing the girls firsthand what they could achieve. A friend and teammate of Maddy's said of her contributions,

> The life of Maddy English is one from which we can all draw great example. As a teacher, she passed along the value of higher education. She had the courage to leave home in 1943 at a young age to play professional baseball at a time when our society was highly skeptical of the ability of women to influence society as popular culture role models. She was an exceptional model.[19]

Much of Everett, Massachusetts, agreed. Maddy English was honored when the town's new middle school was named for her. The school board ran a contest asking students to submit essays detailing who they should name the school after and why. An eighth-grade student of Maddy's, Tiffani Macarelli, wrote the winning essay. It eloquently sums up Maddy's role in the revolution in women's sports:

> I believe the new Lewis school should be named the Maddy English School in honor of Maddy English.... First of all, [she] played professional baseball which, at that time, was considered a "man's sport." By playing a so-called "man's" sport, Maddy showed that she had the confidence in herself.... She became a professional third baseman because she practiced hard and was determined to play for the pros.... I believe the school should be named the Maddy English School not only because she shows determination, confidence, and intelligence and is well-rounded, but also because to her, the sky is the limit.... I believe that this attitude and these characteristics are the key to success in life. As you can see Maddy English is not only a role model to sports fans, but to people of all

ages and interests. Maddy English shows many great qualities and shows that
being a team player is the best kind of person to be in life.[20]

Maddy's legacy, stemming from her time playing professional
baseball, clearly reached far beyond the playing field. Both as a baseball
player and as a teacher, she had the opportunity to touch the lives of
many young people. Maddy's experiences after the league and the obvious impact she had on her students provide but one example of how
seriously former players took their position as role models.

Few women represent the ways in which former players became
role models through education better than Katie Horstman (1951–
1954). In the 1960s, she graduated from Medical Record Librarian
School. She later joined the Franciscan Sisters of the Sacred Heart reli-
gious order. While there, she became the first nun in the United States
to earn a bachelor of science degree in physical education. For the next
decade, Katie taught physical education in Illinois, Indiana, and Ohio
before returning to her hometown of Minster, where she initiated programs in several girls' sports, including volleyball, gymnastics, basketball, track and field, cross country, and softball. "I could not believe
that girls had nothing," she explained. "No sports at all. It was unfair
and I was determined."[21] By 1980, Katie was focused on coaching track
and cross country. Over the next five years, her girls' teams never lost
a track meet. In total, her teams won seven state high school track
meets and were the runners-up four times. They also won a state high
school cross country championship, all twelve track and five cross
country conference meets, and eleven track and two cross country district and regional championships. Katie also coached twenty-nine individual state high school track champions.[22]

Katie was widely recognized by the Minster, Ohio, school system
for her coaching skills and for opening doors for women in sports. But
Katie's success as a coach cannot be measured simply by the number
of titles or wins. Her legacy also includes her work ethic, her leadership,
her desire for perfection, and her love for the Minster girls, which continue even today. Former Minster athletes who were coached by Katie
have made that clear: "She taught me discipline and passion for whatever I did." "She kindled a passion for running that has carried with me

as a lifelong runner and a coach." "She taught me how to discipline myself to make sacrifices to truly go after what I wanted to achieve." High praise from her student athletes, but none more important than this one:

> Miss Horstman didn't coddle; she pushed and pulled. She didn't pamper; she challenged. She demanded your attention, she demanded your commitment, she demanded your effort, and in doing so earned your respect and love. She disciplined with love and you loved the discipline.[23]

Katie Horstman demanded total effort from her students and generally got it because she also provided them with an example of what such determination and commitment to sports could bring in all aspects of life.

Like Katie, Jean Cione (1945–1954) became a lifelong role model for the students whose lives she touched. Jean was born in Rockford, Illinois, and, like so many of her teammates, was the only girl on a boys'

Left to right: Jean Cione (former player) and associate member of the AAGPBL-PA, Ginny Hunt (photograph by Cami J. Kidder).

softball team. In 1942, Jean became the first girl to letter in a sport at Rock River School.[24] Her professional baseball career began in 1945 when she tried out for Max Carey in Rockford. At age seventeen, she was selected and assigned to the Rockford Peaches. Her baseball career was very successful, but she agreed that the time she spent in the league was perhaps most important in that it "served as a template for my vocation and avocation throughout my life."[25] Like so many of the other former players, Jean understood that her time playing professional baseball established a foundation for her future. It gave her confidence, an income, and the ability to dream bigger.

After the league ended, Jean completed her college degree and became a high school teacher. She assumed many responsibilities during her ten years of teaching; among other things, she established and chaired a physical education department, and, as a synchronized swimming specialist, she directed many student synchronized swimming shows. But, as was true when she was a student, there were few competitive athletic opportunities for girls and therefore no coaching positions. However, Jean's career changed dramatically with the passage of Title IX. In the early 1970s, Jean became the first women's athletic director at Eastern Michigan University.[26] In order to comply with the new federal regulations on gender equity, the university charged Jean with creating a women's athletic program. She guided the new program through its initial growth process, and then she returned to teaching in the university's sports medicine curriculum. Jean's impact on young girls and women is immeasurable. Countless female athletes continue to benefit from athletics at Eastern Michigan University because of the work she put into building the women's athletic program, but even more learned about strength, independence and personal security by having her as a role model.

From playing baseball on the streets of her neighborhood to founding an Olympic Training Center, Karen Violetta Kunkel (1952) is one of the best examples of how women from the AAGPBL helped to carve out a place for women's sports in the narrative of American history. Every aspect of her life demonstrates how the AAGPBL players have made a difference in the revolution in women's sports. Karen was born in Negaunee, in Michigan's Upper Peninsula, in 1934. She was one of three children and an only daughter, and, like other AAGPBL players, she was a self-described tomboy who played baseball with the neighborhood boys. Always a good athlete but with no options for sports in high school, Karen played softball on amateur teams in Marquette. After graduating from high school, Karen attended Michigan State University, where she eventually earned two degrees.

Karen was an exceptional athlete. As a college student, she played in the women's NCAA lacrosse tournament and qualified for the men's ski team. In 1953, Karen finished second in the women's downhill at a meet in Cadillac, Michigan. Two years later, in 1955, she won the women's downhill skiing championship in another competition at Cadillac. During the interval between those two events, she played baseball for the Grand Rapids Chicks of the AAGPBL as a utility infielder. She embodied all that a female athlete could be in that time period. Still, as a woman, Karen faced discrimination. She was not, for example, allowed to compete on the men's ski team because of her gender. Rather than accept defeat, she vowed revenge. That feistiness would shape her professional career and make her an important force in changing opportunities for female athletes.

After the league ended, Karen joined the physical education faculty at Northern Michigan University. Frustrated by the lack of knowledge about athletes' health, she promoted the idea of a sports health academy, which eventually secured funding in 1982. Remembering her vow, she also helped start the women's national collegiate ski championships under the sponsorship of the Association of Intercollegiate Athletics for Women (AIAW). No girl would be denied the opportunity to ski as she had been. In addition, Karen served as a director of the AIAW championships, as a member of the organization's National Ski Board, and on the board of directors of the Midwest Collegiate Ski Association.[27]

Karen's influence even extended to the international level. Perhaps her greatest achievement in sports was organizing and administering the U.S. Olympics Training Center at Northern Marquette University in 1985. The center operated in cooperation with other centers at Colorado Springs and Lake Placid and provided athletes and coaches with a place to train and do research, as well as the opportunity for educational advancement. It was the only Olympic facility in the nation that combined athletic training with schooling. In combination with the Great Lakes Sports Training Center, also administered by Karen, it offered internship programs in sports journalism and sports management and administration. Karen retired from her position in 1988.

Even after retirement, Karen's influence on sports continued. She became one of the founders of the AAGPBL Players Association and served as a technical advisor on the 1992 movie *A League of Their Own*. During her work on the movie, she helped test different actresses for skills needed to play the sport and provided information on the types of uniforms the players wore and some of the baseball terms and language used at the time. Karen's continued passion for sports and her dedication to women's sports is evident in her life after the league and in all that she achieved in opening doors for future generations of female athletes.

The women who played for the AAGPBL were part of the women's sports revolution in many ways. Through their bravery in becoming professional athletes in a period when this was not socially sanctioned behavior, in continuing to play sports throughout their lives, and in advocating for female athletics in their professional and volunteer lives, they helped expand the possibilities for girls who wanted to play ball. But their most significant contribution was as role models. The players were, and continue to be, heroes to young girls. Their example demonstrates to future female athletes that it is all right to be a woman *and* be strong and athletic. It shows them that women in the past fought against discrimination and limited options and emerged triumphant. It gives girls a model to emulate, opening doors to the self-confidence, determination, and positive sense of self that sports can foster.

But what makes the former AAGPBL players true revolutionaries is their recognition that just being there at the beginning was not enough. As Jeanne DesCombes Lesko (1953–1954) put it, "we have to support other girls in sports." They understood that the legacy of the league is not stagnant; rather, it continues to grow along with the influence of the players.

> I don't think anybody knew who we were until the movie came out. So, we didn't think we were anybody special. No matter who you talk to, we said that we played for the love of the game because we loved to play the game. And constantly we

Left to right: Jeneane DesCombes Lesko, Toni Palermo, and Helen "Sis" Waddell. As always, ready to take the field (photograph by Cami J. Kidder).

would go as a group someplace and people are telling us "Gee if it hadn't been for you there wouldn't have been any Title IX," well that's not true. Bill[ie] Jean King probably did more for Title IX than anybody in women's sports. But in retrospect all history is based like that on what people did previously, so we have kind of inherited that position and I think that since we have inherited it we have done more for it consciously than we did before; I mean I don't think anybody had any thought of women in the future while we were playing. But now the position that we are in we support other girls in sports we are always all out going to schools, not all of us but a good portion of the women have been in sports all of these years in one capacity or another as teachers, instructors, or coaches they all have added to it throughout their lifetimes.[28]

For Lesko, as for many of the other former players, being part of the revolution of women in sports became a lifetime commitment.

That long-term commitment is still necessary. The progress made in women's sports over the last few decades is impressive, but, as is suggested by my students' questions about the relevance of Title IX, we have a long way to go. There is much work left to do before the importance and influence of women's sports are truly understood and appreciated. The AAGPBL demonstrated that women could definitely play baseball, a man's game. Despite the fact that they were making history, at the time most of the women in the league did not think about that fact. In hindsight, however, the players understand what they did and are aware of their legacy, their "true place in American history." Betsy "Sock 'em" Jochum (1943–1948) agreed: "I guess we were pioneers, patriots and trailblazers. Are those all the same thing? Doesn't matter, we were, and still are all of those things."[29]

5

Life After:
The Reconnection

"I just never knew how much they meant to me until I saw them again. Oh, what a coming home."
—Terry Donahue[1]

At the first reunion of the All-American Girls Professional Baseball League, pitcher Maybelle Blair (1948) and catcher Terry Donahue (1946–1949) met for what Terry thought was the first time. But when a photographer called for the 1948 Peoria Redwings to line up for a picture, both women stood up. Terry, always outspoken, cried, "Who are you?"

"I was a pitcher in 1948," Blair answered. "You were my catcher."

"I don't remember ever catching *your* curves," Terry said wryly.

They both laughed. Since that time, the two women have been family to each other.

Similar stories of rediscovery and connection are heard over and over at the yearly reunions of the AAGPBL. Former players just seem to understand each other. And even though they had very different lives after playing professional ball, the connections they forged on the baseball diamond some forty years earlier have provided the foundation for renewed friendship and loyalty, and for comfort and support as they aged. They became powers of attorney for each other, offered support when spouses or children died, cared for each other at the end of their lives, and, no matter what, remained teammates. But what happened in those intervening years? How did the players lose each other and how did they fare without the closeness they shared during their time in the league? The answers to those questions are as diverse as the players themselves.

The All-American Girls After the AAGPBL

Isabel "Lefty" Alvarez (1949–1954) played softball on leagues at General Electric, where she worked for more than 30 years. Few of her company teammates knew about her baseball past or that she had been part of a professional women's baseball league. In fact, they were unaware that there had been a league at all. They were not alone in their ignorance. Most of the country was in the dark. "Even if I did try to talk about playing baseball," Lefty told me, "people would say, 'you mean softball, women don't play baseball.'"[2] That comment was repeated thousands of times to nearly every ball player who tried to discuss her experience in the AAGPBL. Eventually many of them simply stopped trying.

It wasn't just a matter of public forgetfulness, however. The players themselves recognize that even *they* did not realize they were making history when they played for the AAGPBL. It was, for many of them, simply the time of their lives. When asked by an interviewer from Grand Valley State University if she had any idea that she was doing something significant, Shirley Burkovich (1949–1951) responded:

> You know when we—when I first went into the league, I thought that this had to be the greatest thing that ever happened to me and I didn't care about anything except playing and having that opportunity, so as far as thinking to myself that this is something special, I never did. In fact until the day [I] left the league, I never thought it was anything special, I didn't see any need to talk about it or tell anybody.... Most people thought it was softball and everything, so it was just never anything that was brought up in conversations.[3]

Maybelle Blair (1948) agreed that while they played, they simply loved the game and did not think about the historical significance of their actions. She thought that this was due in part to the players' belief that the league would never end.

But there was more to it than that. It was easy to discount the league's existence because people tend to see sports as less important than careers, families or other accomplishments, and this is especially true for girls and women. For the women themselves, it was difficult to see the historical significance because they were simply doing what they enjoyed, and because having the chance to play baseball was to them a rare and fleeting opportunity. Once it ended they went on with their lives and rarely spoke about that time. The result of this collective amnesia was a 30-year gap during which players lost track of one another and nearly lost their place in both baseball history and U.S. history. Their road back to each other and to public recognition was long, but, as Lefty said, "It was well worth the wait. I have my family back now and people know what we did. Finally."[4]

Widespread recognition of the league did come with the release of the movie *A League of Their Own* in 1992, but the players' road back to each other began much earlier. The desire, even need, to find their teammates was an important step in the eventual recognition of the league. It was that desire, combined with the lasting connection between the players and their host families, that led to the first reunion. For many of the players, host families they were assigned to by the league were just that—family. Host families were often fans of the local team who had room for one or two of the players. Some, however, were connected to the league in other ways at first, opening their homes to players later. Arnold Bauer, an usher for the South Bend Blue Sox, and his wife housed a number of the players. It was Bauer and his partner, Ed Des Lauriers, who first set out to "find our girls," many of whom responded.[5] Des Lauriers and Bauer sent out more than 400 letters to former players and got 148 replies.[6] The high number of responses is an indication of just how excited the players were reconnect with that part of their past. The survey asked about the players' families, about marriage and children, and whether they went back to school or went to work. It also inquired about their continued interest and participation in sports. In their responses, former players

Former player Sue Kidd.

expressed fond memories of their time in the league, and many mentioned the idea of holding a reunion. Neither Des Lauriers or Bauer followed up on the suggestion. They sent a composite of their findings to the respondents but did little else with the information.

The desire of the players to reunite was helped along by the growth of women's studies classes in colleges during the 1970s; students began researching all aspects of women's history, including women's sports history.[7] After reading Merrie Fidler's master's thesis, "The Development and Decline of the All-American Girls Professional Baseball League," scholar Sharon Roepke began researching and writing about the league as well. During her research, Roepke visited the National Baseball Hall of Fame, and when she found virtually nothing about women, she started asking questions. Administrators of the hall initially ignored her inquiries, but Roepke continued to ask why they had ignored the contributions of women in baseball. Eventually, her efforts

Toni Palermo signing a bat for baseball umpire Perry Barber—two generations of women in baseball (photograph by Cami J. Kidder).

paid off. The Hall of Fame began creating files on women in baseball and finally took notice of the AAGPBL. It was Roepke who helped bring the league to the attention of the sports history world, as she presented her research at a number of Society for American Baseball Research (SABR) and North American Society of Sport History meetings.[8]

At around the same time, without even knowing that Roepke and others were researching the history of the league, former players started seeking each other out. During a visit with June Peppas (1948–1954) at her Michigan home, Dorothy "Kammie" Kamenshek (1943–1953) and Marge Wenzell (1945–1953) reminisced about former players and wondered if a reunion was possible. The three of them, who had remained close friends, and their quest for other players, became the catalyst for the first reunion.

Over the years since the league ended, Peppas had collected the addresses of as many players as she could find. She combined these

Catcher Lois Youngen in the National Baseball Hall of Fame sculpture garden with the statue of catcher Roy Campanella (photograph by Cami J. Kidder).

with the addresses that Kamenshek and Wenzell had and, taking advantage of owning a printing company, sent letters to all of them. In those letters, Peppas mentioned the possibility of a reunion and asked for each person to respond with as much information about other players as possible.[9] The response was terrific, and with the information she received, Peppas was able to send out a newsletter in January 1981.

The first newsletter consisted of one typed page, but the impact was powerful. In February 1981, Peppas sent another newsletter because, as she stated, "Our response last month was fantastic ... so decided that another issue was in order." This edition went to 130 individuals and was, in the opinion of Peppas, the "first real newsletter."[10] In this newsletter Peppas requested more information about former players and urged her readers to report back about their lives after the league. The response to this letter was even greater than before, and another was sent out in March 1981. Unlike the earlier newsletters, which were primarily requests for players' contact information, the March letter included not only more addresses but also an "In Memory of..." section and old photographs of their days in the league. This was the first edition of the newsletter to include newspaper clippings, and the first time Peppas began to call seriously for a national reunion. An edition of the newsletter went out nearly every month after that. For the players, the journey back to each other began in earnest.

In the summer of 1981, Peppas hosted a picnic for former players at her home in Michigan. Because of the success of that event, she reported in the next newsletter, "We plan on lots more gatherings in the very near future."[11] A few of the former South Bend Blue Sox also organized their own reunion, which took place in August 1981. And then, in September of that year, the Fort Wayne Women's Bureau sponsored an event called "Run, Jane Run—Women in Sports." The event was a celebration of women in all sports, but the former Fort Wayne Daisies in the area used the event as an opportunity to come together. There was a three-inning exhibition game between the former players and the developmental players known during the league's existence as Junior Daisies. Sharon Roepke presented a slide show about the league, and other women provided scrapbooks for reminiscing. It was on that September weekend that the plans for a national reunion really began to take shape. By September 1981, the overwhelming theme of the newsletters was the former players' desire to reunite. In the "Letters" column of the newsletter many players wrote longingly about a reunion. Most did not even bother to argue that there should be one but simply offered ideas about where to hold it.[12]

Ruth Davis (1952–1954), a South Bend Blue Sox bat girl, volunteered to lead the way in organizing the gathering. Although many of the players voiced the concern that it would be too difficult to organize a national event, Davis believed that the league itself gave her not only the motivation to organize the reunion but also the strength to make it happen.

> I think ... perhaps that is the greatest legacy of the League, that it presented a Model for all of us growing up at that time that we could do whatever we set our minds to—because we didn't know that we couldn't. We saw women who were participating in a sport where women had never played before (professionally). We saw those same women go on to become pioneers in physical therapy, medicine, aviation, education, law. We saw some of them become rich, some dedicate their lives to the poor, to the church, and to humanity. The women who played in the League were not just great athletes; they were the best this country had to offer in so many ways.... I know that not everyone fell into that mold, but if I were a statistician, I'll bet that the greats outweighed the not so greats at a statistically higher rate than in the general public.[13]

Davis' "can-do" spirit, along with Peppas' newsletter, made the reunion possible.

The first national reunion of the All-American Girls Professional Baseball League was set for July 1982 in Chicago. Because Philip Wrigley, owner of the Chicago Cubs, had created the league, and because many of the former players still lived in the Midwest, Chicago was the logical place. The four-day gathering included a number of events, such as a Chicago Cubs game, a golf outing and a banquet. But it was the reminiscing, the catching up, that made the trip worthwhile for many of the former players:

> It was a beautiful experience to be part of the reunion of so many wonderful people.... The lobby became the scene of the world's biggest love-in! If it never happens again, it happened this once—a reunion to be duplicated and always to be remembered in everyone's hearts—Forever.[14]

Despite the fears that this would be a once-in-a-lifetime event, reunions continued. The next one was planned for Fort Wayne in 1986;

then another took place in Scottsdale, Arizona, in October 1988. Each reunion was different and drew different players, but the sense that they had to continue was strong. Players' shared sense of history, of experiences only they could understand, and their pride in what they had accomplished bonded them, and once they were physically reconnected most were determined to never lose that connection again.

The way back to one another had been long, but, for many of the women, reconnecting with teammates at the players' reunions was life altering. The memories Audrey Daniels (1944–1951) shared about her time in the league demonstrate the sense of friendship and camaraderie between the players and exactly why it was so important for former players to reconnect:

> It taught me a lot. It taught me to be considerate. And, listen, I was one of them that learned how to pour tea and you ever need someone to pour tea at some of your social events or walk with a book on my head, I can do that too. Of course we accomplished more than playing baseball, we showed that we were as equal as boys. Coming into sports and giving the women's sports the same consideration that you're giving the boys and we did you know, chapter nine [Title IX] was passed for equal opportunity in sports and I think we accomplished a great deal and we're proud of what we did, we're very proud of it. Really, though even more important than that, in some ways, is the love of all of my friends here [at the reunion], because they're like more than just friends and some of them you probably think are your family you know.[15]

Audrey was not alone in her belief that the friendship—the family—they created along the way was the most important benefit of their time in the league. While Beans Risinger played in the AAGPBL, she made many friends who became a surrogate family. The reunions allowed her to rediscover and maintain those relationships for the rest of her lifetime. Those friends, along with her baseball experiences, taught Beans that it did not matter where a person came from or how rich or poor they might be. Rather, it is how you react to those circumstances that defines a person's worth.

For Lefty, making friends in the league was complicated by her shyness and the language barrier. Her story vividly illustrates why the reunions were so crucial for many of the players. When she first played for the league, Lefty experienced a great deal of loneliness and isolation. "It was hard for people to know my feelings, and sometimes they took things for granted, like how important they were to me, I never could tell them," she remembered.[16] She often felt like she "was in a cloud," unable to understand or communicate. Fortunately, Lefty began her career with the Chicago Colleens, known as the touring team and full of younger, less experienced players. Baseball became a common language. "Those people are still my friends," she said. "And they are the ones who helped me and taught me. When I was lonely they talked to me about baseball, and that I could understand. It made me feel less stupid and less alone."[17] Ultimately, the Colleens gave Lefty the sense of family and security she desperately needed. Lefty was able to connect to people, learn English and develop lifelong friendships. "I left family for family," she said, "the other players teased me a lot but only because they liked me."

Once the league ended, Lefty was left with no "family" and no support system. She spent 30 years working at General Electric, and despite the fact that she worked alongside the same people for many of those years, she felt lonely and isolated. Because she lacked formal education and was embarrassed by her strong Cuban accent, Lefty did not seek advancements at GE or try to make friends. "Just because of my accent people did not think I was intelligent," she said. "I could talk, but my words were more or less backward, you know, mixed up, and they'd think I was dumb."[18]

Marie "Red" Mahoney, who was inducted into the Texas Baseball Hall of Fame in 2006. While the league as a whole was recognized by the National Baseball Hall of Fame in 1988, individual players have been honored by many state and local organizations.

To help handle the loneliness and the difficulties of life after baseball, Lefty started drinking heavily and smoking, things she never did during her playing days: "I was not homesick, probably just depressed and did not realize it. The drinking only made it worse, as I know now. I had no security then, was all alone and unsure how to handle so many things." Lefty was unsettled, and she jumped from one place to the other, staying with acquaintances for brief periods, often scared and panicked in the mornings about how she had gotten home. She had a number of car accidents and totaled two cars before she stopped drinking. "I was very lucky that I did not get killed or kill someone while driving drunk," she said.[19]

The rediscovery of her baseball family through the reunions was an important beginning to Lefty's recovery. No doubt alcohol masked the fear and loneliness in her life, and even now she credits her faith and baseball for stopping the downward spiral. It was sports and what she learned during her career as a baseball player, as well as the relationships with her teammates, that ultimately saved her: "I was going down. Drinking, smoking. Going down. Then I thought about baseball and how I felt when I played. It helped me, but what really helped was when I saw them again. Holy cow."[20] Reconnecting with her baseball family was crucial in helping Lefty beat back her demons. Her old friends, many of whom had lived all those years just a few miles away from her, became a new support system. Because they had similar baseball experiences and instinctively understood the role of baseball in Lefty's life, they encouraged her to talk about that time, to relive it and feel proud because of it. With rekindled friendships and a renewed sense of pride in her baseball career, Lefty was able to overcome her drinking problem and the loneliness it masked. The other factor that made a difference for Lefty was that she, and her teammates, became famous.

The reunions reunited the players and rekindled old friendships, but they also helped to put the league back in the public eye. An event connected to the second reunion would start them on the road to celebrity. While the players were planning the reunion, to be held in Fort Wayne, Indiana, in 1986, Kelly Candaele and Kim Wilson began work on a documentary they called *A League of Their Own*. Candaele was the son of former player Helen Callaghan, and Wilson was a film

Casey Candaele (left) talking with Terry Donahue (right). Casey's brother Kelly Candaele's PBS documentary about the AAGPBL led to the creation of the 1992 film, *A League of Their Own*, directed by Penny Marshall. Candaele's mother, Helen Callaghan, played in the AAGPBL; Terry was one of Helen's teammates.

maker. Candaele began taping interviews with such California players as Faye Dancer (1945–1947), Thelma "Tiby" Eisen (1944–1952), and his mother, Helen Callaghan Candaele (1944–1949). Kelly wanted to "share a part of my Mom's life that I had heard about growing up and to honor her experience and achievements."[21] His documentary was based on interviews, film footage from the National Archives, and many pictures and keepsakes from the players themselves. A Public Broadcast System (PBS) station agreed to pay for a director and to fly a production team to Fort Wayne to film the reunion. The film aired nationwide in September 1987. No one, certainly not the players, had any idea that the documentary would become the basis for a major motion picture. But only a few months after the debut of the documentary, movie producers sought out the organization. In 1988, the board of directors signed a contract with Longbow Productions of California.

Though they were excited about the film, the players also sought other avenues of recognition. During the Scottsdale reunion in 1988, the players began, in earnest, to push for recognition by the National Baseball Hall of Fame, located in Cooperstown, New York. Pepper Paire reminded the players that while it was a good thing to be remembered in film, there was a lot left to do.

> Pretty fantastic, huh gals?? We will be immortalized on celluloid for the future! ... Perhaps a film on the AAGPBL might be the trumpet to topple the Walls of the Great Hall of Fames of Baseball! ... Where does it say "Mens" Baseball Hall of Fame?[22]

Recognition by the Hall of Fame became a priority, so, as they had done as players, the women worked together to create the All-American Girls Professional Baseball League Players Association. The association became the public face and force of their efforts to gain recognition. Former players wrote letters to the Hall of Fame, contacted the president and the curators, and sought to ascertain the amount of memorabilia that still existed for donation to the hall for an exhibit. And after a great deal of negotiation (and stubbornness), their efforts paid off. Ted Spencer, the Hall of Fame's curator, began communicating with representatives of the league in 1986, and shortly after that he entered into negotiations to get the AAGPBL players recognized by the hall. Spencer assured the group that they wanted to do an exhibit, but space and a lack of memorabilia were concerns.[23] Once assured that there would be no problem with finding items to display, and with Spencer's full support, serious negotiations between the HOF and the AAGPBL began.

Many of the league members did not want a display, nor did they want to share an exhibit with other women in baseball. Instead, they wanted the entire league to be inducted into the hall as a single honorary member, which would include a ceremony and full recognition. While most of the players understood that many women had played, coached and umpired baseball outside the AAGPBL, they argued that their group was the first professional women's league and should therefore have a special place in the Hall of Fame. Further, players wanted to ensure that the exhibit would be permanent and not simply a one-time event. Maintaining that the hall could not *induct* a whole league, as such an action went against its historical mission, Spencer proposed a compromise: there would be a "Women in Baseball" exhibit, and the hall would hold an unveiling ceremony to honor the women. After a great deal of discussion and disagreement, the membership agreed to this proposal, and the date was set for the league's recognition by the National Baseball Hall of Fame.[24]

One hundred fifty former players from the AAGPBL, along with countless friends and family members, met in Cooperstown on November 3, 1988, for the three-day event. Former player (and the person who kept the dream of Hall of Fame recognition alive) Dottie Collins and Hall of Fame president Howard Talbot pulled the cord to unveil the "Women in Baseball" exhibit. As Ted Spencer remembered years later,

> Here's a day where we [normally] have 400 people. That's what we'd have on a Saturday in November, 400 people. [But t]he place was packed, and they sang that [AAGPBL] song all day long.... And this museum had never had that much noise! It was great.... To me it changed the whole direction of the museum because it brought home how important the game is culturally.[25]

One of the attendees at the Hall of Fame event, "hidden in plain sight behind sunglasses and a baseball cap," was popular Hollywood director Penny Marshall. She was there chasing a story for a new film. "One day," she recalled later, "I saw a documentary on the All American Girls Professional Baseball League of the 1940s. It was about a group of courageous women who were recruited to play baseball when the young men who played ball had gone off to fight World War II."[26] Excited by the history, she secured the rights to the story, and to the use of Kelly Candaele and Kim Wilson's title, and began unofficial work on a movie that would have the same name as the documentary. Hearing about the Hall of Fame recognition, she jumped at the chance to meet the players. Marshall attended many of the events that weekend, and she left with renewed determination to make a movie about these women. For Marshall, this wasn't just another story. She explained that she "chose to direct *A League of Their Own* because I thought it was a story that needed to be told, and told with accuracy, inspiration and humor."[27] In the end, Marshall would be more successful than she could have ever dreamed possible.

Penny Marshall's respect for the players is evident in her decision

Former players Maybelle Blair (left) and Shirley Burkovich (right) coaching the girls at the 2015 Baseball for All tournament, the first all-girls national baseball tournament, Orlando, Florida.

to include them in the making of the film. Some worked as advisors, doing everything from offering suggestions about period dress to coaching Hollywood stars on how to throw a baseball. Many of the former players were present in the scenes at the end of the movie showcasing the Cooperstown event. Most did not have speaking parts in the movie, but those who did still get royalty checks. Shirley Burkovich proudly cashes a check for $1.97 every month for her line, "Dottie, having you here is good luck."[28] The experience of being in the movie was fun and, as Shirley put it, "the icing on an already tasty cake."[29]

On July 4, 1992, *A League of Their Own* opened the eyes of the

Left to right: Pat Henschel (associate member AAGPBL-PA), Maybelle Blair (former player), and Terry Donahue (former player), in Maui, Hawaii. These women travel together, play together, and take care of each other.

world to the women of the AAGPBL and their story. The movie, now a cultural phenomenon, is shown almost daily on cable television, and young girls recite lines from the movie as if it were current. Finally, after nearly forty years, women's professional baseball had reentered the American consciousness.

The former players are very aware that without the movie their time as professional baseball players would likely have gone unnoticed. Terry Donahue argues that, if not for the movie, "we would have all been dead and gone and no one would have ever known about us." When asked about whether her playing days were known, she said,

> No, I never talked about it. Nobody knew that I had played professional ball. If I had told them they probably thought that I was crazy, so let me tell you, when that movie started all hell broke loose. They wanted to interview me, television and radio. It was incredible but very exciting.... Well we were I know I was very

excited to think that this movie was going to tell our story, which is something we love doing. We didn't know how it was going to come out. We were very worried until we saw it, but when we saw it we were very pleased. I remember going to Rockford to see the movie for the first time with all of the girls there and we had tears, we were really excited. And except for that movie nobody would have known about it.[30]

In a stinging rejoinder to a film critic, one former player, Patricia Brown (1950–1951), showed exactly why the movie mattered so much. The critic, whom Brown refuses to mention, had overlooked the significance of the movie, calling it "a pseudo–Norman Rockwell slice of Americana." He also said that the women were "all clichés in uniform." In her book, *A League of My Own*, Brown reprinted the letter she published in response:

Mr. [she leaves out his name] misses the point of the film entirely. He wants to add today's lifestyles to yesterday's history. While he calls the women characters "clichés in uniforms," Penny Marshall shows how women were given a chance to do something unique in history, something previously only available to men, playing baseball, and playing it well! It gave us confidence in our lives and in our future careers. I myself went on to become a lawyer and earn four degrees. I guess I was a cliché in uniform.[31]

Brown could have spoken for nearly every one of the women who played in the league.

Of course, as Maybelle Blair has pointed out, the film could never have happened unless the women themselves had started the process.

Nobody [knew about the AAGPBL], nobody did until after the movie. The movie was the making of everybody and even when you mention[ed] that you played in the all American or the National league they [didn't] know what you [were] talking about and could care less, now they care, it's amazing. We wouldn't have the movie though if we hadn't had those reunions. That really got us going.[32]

Since the film came out, the league's fame has continued to grow. Dozens of articles and books have been written about it. Scores of individual players have been inducted into local halls of fame, and in 2006 a statue representing the league was unveiled at the National Baseball Hall of Fame in Cooperstown. The sculpture is located in what is known as Cooper Park, and it stands just a few yards away from existing statues honoring the 1955 Brooklyn Dodgers' World Series championship and

Hall of Famer Satchel Paige. Nearly 50 former players were present when the statue was unveiled, and even at that point, 63 years after the league began and 14 years after the debut of the movie, they were excited, humbled and proud of the recognition.

In telling the story of the AAGPBL, the film also changed the lives of the league's players. For many, it opened doors to travel, write and, of course, engage in public speaking. To some of the players, the idea that they might write a book, speak before large crowds, or be interviewed for television or radio once seemed farfetched. After the release of the movie, however, that is exactly what happened. The players travel all over the country, speaking and signing autographs, and they have been interviewed countless times on television and radio programs, including CBS's *Sunday Morning.* Terry Donahue remembered how overwhelming it was for them at first:

Mary Moore (left) and Sarah Jane "Salty" Ferguson (right) posing with the AAGPBL statue outside the National Baseball Hall of Fame, Cooperstown, New York.

> When that [the movie] came out, and the people at work couldn't believe it, that I had played professional [baseball]. So it was pretty exciting, oh goodness gracious. You know we were being interviewed, we weren't talkers and we would never, it was incredible. People just wanted, I said well if you want an interview come to my apartment because we were running around like crazy, we all were. We were overwhelmed, really. We couldn't believe that we were getting all of this attention. Because anytime you mention that movie people go crazy. I think we were really overwhelmed and so excited.[33]

Wilma Briggs (1948–1954) agreed that the movie "did wonders for spreading the word about our league." And that visibility changed her life in unexpected ways: "I've been inducted into 5 halls of fame. I was named 15 out of 50 of Rhode Island's Greatest Sports Figures from 1900–2000 by *Sports Illustrated*."[34] Most of the players follow the mantra "all for one and one for all," but these individual honors were also important and gave the women a greater sense of pride and accomplishment.

Most of the players dealt with the newfound popularity just fine, and even flourished because of it. For Lefty Alvarez, it was especially transformative. Initially, she found it hard to convince friends of forty years that she had been "one of those ball players." Although she had worked on the movie set and even appeared in the film's final scene, her friends and coworkers still did not believe Lefty when she quietly announced that she had played in the league. But she *had* been "one of those ball players," a fact that changed her life forever. When asked about why her coworkers didn't know about her career as a ball player, Lefty said, "I've always been shy. I never wanted to talk to people but now, holy cow, people want to know my story all the time. So, I tell them." Lefty's experience is echoed by Beans Risinger: "I was a kid from Hess, Oklahoma, I am not comfortable with speaking in public, just never did it. But, after the movie, we were contacted by lots of people who asked for interviews so I had to learn." Both Lefty and Beans have had articles written about them, have been interviewed many times, and have appeared on television and in documentaries. These are experiences neither would have had if their careers as professional athletes had not been portrayed in a popular movie.

While the players love the personal recognition they got from the movie, their greatest satisfaction comes from the opportunity to talk about women's sports that the movie provided. In her book about the

5. *Life After: The Reconnection*

history of the league, Merrie Fidler put this idea especially well: "The film revealed a concept that is still just beginning to emerge in this country. It revealed that there is meaning and importance to girls' and women's participation in sport."[35] In this way, the film strengthened the players' role as a bridge between women's sports history and the future of women's sports. And they became very aware of that role and the responsibility that comes with being pioneers. Because people, especially young women, began looking up to them, seeking them out and wanting desperately to be like them, players took on what many believe to be a serious responsibility—teaching children, especially girls, about sports.

Beans Risinger spent a great deal of time coaching girls and talking to them about the importance of sports and why girls should play them. Like many of the players, Beans used the fame created by the movie to encourage girls to follow their dreams.

> We feel that we helped women get to play more sports etc. by us doing that because when I first came to Grand Rapids and stayed in the wintertime, I said, "What do the girls get to do in high school and around [here]"? Well, they didn't get to do anything and I feel now that softball is so great now, that we were stepping stones for the younger generation.... We feel like we made our mark in that respect.[36]

Like Beans, Shirley Burkovich and Maybelle Blair recognized that their fame gave them a unique opportunity to talk about sports, the importance of playing but also the ways in which sports provided further educational opportunities for girls.

> We [Shirley and Maybelle] started working with other ex–major league ball players on free clinics for girls and boys. The clinics used to be strictly for the boys, and then we started going out and saying in these clinics "girls and boys," and there was a group of us, some ex-Dodgers and ex-Angels, that they put together this group called Sports Educators of America, and we went out, this was just in the Southern California area, and we would go out and do these free baseball clinics for the kids and we would try to incorporate education and sports. Telling the kids that education is just as important because you ask the kids, "Who wants to be a major league ball player?" Well, everybody raises their hand, so then you say to them, "Well, all right, there are 700 positions in major league baseball, what if you don't make it, then what?" So we tell them that they've got to have something to fall back on, so we start stressing education in sports to these kids, trying to encourage them to stay in school and have a back-up just in case they don't make it in the baseball world. I can always relate

115

to that because that's what happened to me. I thought baseball was always going to be my career and I didn't plan for anything else. Fortunately, I got a job at the telephone company and at that time the companies were more like families. The telephone company was like a family, so I had the opportunity to work for them, so that's what we have been doing now for the last ten or fifteen years, going out to these clinics and working with young people.[37]

Young people all over the country have taken the women's message to heart. Sports are no longer seen as just a place for boys, and we now have opportunities in sports as a cause worth fighting for because, as the women of the AAGPBL demonstrate, if given a chance to play, the lives of girls will forever be changed. They will learn to win and lose, to have confidence in themselves and, as Beans said, to "shoot for the moon, and if you fail or fall, you will still be among the stars."[38]

Left to right: Carol Sheldon (associate member of the AAGPBL-PA), Jeneane Lesko (former player), Debbie Pierson (associate member), Toni Palermo (former player), and Cami J. Kidder (associate member). At all reunions, players readily interact with fans and associate members of the organization. Once you attend a reunion, you are family (photograph by Cami J. Kidder).

5. Life After: The Reconnection

In 2008 the AAGPBL held its annual reunion on a cruise ship. There were, of course, hundreds of other passengers on the ship, most of whom had only a passing curiosity about the women as they walked around in their AAGPBL hats and shirts. Like most cruise ships, this one was large and had a magnificent central stairway that rose the full three stories of the ship. One evening, as the players waited to enter the dining room, they gathered on the stairs and, with no prompting, began singing the league song. Their voices filled the central portion of the ship, and on all three stories people stopped what they were doing to listen. When it was over there was silence for several seconds as people tried to take in what they had just witnessed, followed by an explosion of applause. The song itself has become iconic and is sung by girls' softball and baseball leagues as they travel by bus from game to game. In June 2015, at the first thirteen-and-under national girls' baseball tournament, former players Maybelle Blair and Shirley Burkovich were honored at the closing ceremonies when they were asked to lead the crowd in singing the song. They began to sing and then stood watching in awe as a crowd of young girls, 8–13 years old, and their parents sang to them. "Wow. They knew the song, all of it, every word," Shirley said, shaking her head.[39]

The film remains an important piece of American culture, one that still reaches female athletes of every age. As Terry Donahue explained in 2008,

> Well even now I don't think that it's changed much since the first time it came out. You mentioned to somebody that you've played and you know they will see my ring and I might be paying a bill or doing something and I'll say "Have you heard of *A League of Their Own*?" and you tell them that you've played they just get so excited. It's incredible.

It took thirty years for the players themselves to find each other again and for people to rediscover the league, but once they did, a force was unleashed. "The rest," as Terry said, "is history." Except that "the rest" has been an all-out effort to retell history, to locate these pioneering athletes in American history—women who made a difference and who helped to pave a path on which future generations could more easily walk. Kristen Huff, an associate member of the players association and a former athlete, vividly recounts the importance of the league to her own life:

The All-American Girls After the AAGPBL

When *A League of Their Own* debuted in 1992, I was not old enough to see it in the movie theater. I spent months eagerly anticipating its arrival on VHS so I could see for my very own eyes: women baseball players. In 1992, I was 9 years old, and at 9 years old in my town, that was the end of your baseball career. That winter, when my mother took me to sign up for Little League, we were approached by the president of all children's athletics in my hometown and told that I would have to sign up for softball. Softball. How would the Cincinnati Reds ever see me if I had to play softball? Though my mother fought for me to stay in Little League baseball, the league president said that it was a league rule that all players had to wear a cup to play baseball. Since I didn't wear a cup, obviously I couldn't play, but we all knew what that meant: when an 8 year old in pigtails reaches over the fence to rob the tallest 9 year old of a homerun, the fathers shove their hands further into their pockets and frown while the mothers stand up and cheer. They couldn't stand for that.

When *A League of Their Own* finally came out on VHS, I watched it continuously. I was validated in my feelings of being a baseball player. I knew that I had been lied to. I searched through stacks and stacks of my baseball cards, never finding a card from any of these players I saw on my television. I wondered why no one had told me that these women existed. I waited until the following winter, when it was time to sign up for Little League again. I marched straight to the table and said, "You are wrong. Women can and did play baseball."

These baseball players never left my mind as I got older. When I was told to stop playing football, or any other activity that "ladies" shouldn't participate in, they were always in the front of my memory. I always told myself that I can do whatever I want to do, regardless of the stigma or gender that society had placed on that activity. When I met the real women of the All American Girls Professional Baseball League as an adult, I was amazed to hear about the things that they had been able to accomplish in their lives. While I am constantly intrigued by all of the personal stories of the women of the league, more importantly to me, they have and will always remain professional baseball players.[40]

The legacy of the All-American Girls Professional Baseball League continues to grow, and with every public appearance by a player, every showing of the movie on cable television, and every new book or article written about the AAGPBL players, their importance to American history is solidified. For the players themselves, however, their place in history is important, but so is their rediscovery of one another. Through finding each other after years apart, they also found a lot more—family.

6

The Next Generation

"Knowing Ms. Maybelle personally and that she has opened up
opportunities for me in future years to continue to play baseball
gives me the power to keep on trying. It gives me the chance to
live a part of her legacy."

—Grace DeVinney

In June 2015, Baseball for All hosted the first girls' national baseball tournament in Orlando, Florida. At the opening ceremony, I sat
with former players from the AAGPBL watching young girls from all
over the United States march into the stadium. Maybelle Blair looked
at me and said, "No matter what else I did, we did, that right there is
the most important thing to come out of the league." In the more than
sixty years since she played with the All-American Girls Professional
Baseball League, Maybelle has witnessed a lot of growth in girls' baseball. But when she watched those girls enter their own tournament,
something began to sink in: "Maybe, just maybe, our real legacy is
them. Not what we did on the field in those years we played, but this.
We helped build this."[1]

History is full of examples of individual women who played baseball. They played with men, or sometimes they played against men on
women's barnstorming teams like the Bloomer Girls or the Dolly Var-
dens. Girls and women have played baseball since the sport was
invented, but rarely in organized leagues of their own. The distinction
of being the first league in which women played against each other
belongs to the All-American Girls Professional Baseball League.
Because of that experience, and the fact that the league became internationally known after the 1992 release of *A League of Their Own*, the
women of the AAGPBL were in a unique position to help build a future

for girls and women in baseball. For many of the players, the efforts to expand girls' baseball took the form of individual coaching and speaking engagements about the league and their experiences in it. For others, it was a lifelong concerted effort to create those opportunities. Regardless of their approach, many women who participated in the league played an important role in the continued growth of girls' and women's baseball through the twentieth century and into the twenty-first.

None of the women of the league would claim that they or the AAGPBL are solely responsible for the growth of girls' baseball, but they do think of themselves as the foundation on which the girls' and women's teams of today were built. Maybelle Blair is quite modest about their contributions:

> All we did was set the stage; then lots of others came after us and built on that foundation. It makes me proud to know that what we did made it possible for women like Ila Borders, Julie Croteau, Justine Siegal, the Colorado Silver Bullets and now the younger girls like Mo'ne Davis and so many others to play baseball.[2]

Former players from the All-American Girls Professional Baseball League take pride in the revolution currently unfolding in girls' and women's baseball. Their connection to that growth is the subject of this chapter. To many of them, nothing is more important to their legacy than this explosion in girls' baseball. They are a living connection to the past and provide the thread that connects the long history of women in baseball to those who play the game today. "We didn't do it all by ourselves," Terry Donahue said, "but we did introduce the thread to the needle."[3] In fact, their contributions are much more than that.

The women themselves helped to create a bridge to modern girls' and women's baseball, beginning almost immediately after the league folded in 1954. During those years, opportunities for girls and women to play baseball were scarce. But Bill Allington, one of the league's most successful coaches, was not willing to give up on women's baseball. Like many of the other coaches, Allington was a former major league ball player and minor league manager. In 1944, he was hired to manage the Rockford Peaches.[4] With Allington in charge, the Peaches reached the playoffs six times and won the AAGPBL championship in 1945, 1948, 1949 and 1950. In 1953 and 1954, Allington managed the Fort

Toni Palermo (left) and Sis Waddell (right) watching the girls take the field at the newly renovated Beyer Stadium in Rockford, Illinois (photograph by Cami J. Kidder).

Wayne Daisies and led them to the playoffs in both seasons. When the league disbanded, Allington formed two women's touring teams called Allington's All-Stars that barnstormed around the country playing men's teams.

The Allington All-Stars played 100 games between 1955 and 1958, traveling nearly 10,000 miles, mostly in the manager's station wagon.[5] Katie Horstman recalled the struggles of travel but claimed, "We were young, we didn't worry too much about the travel. We just wanted to play baseball."[6] Allington's determination provided a few more years of professional baseball for some of the AAGPBL's players, including Katie Horstman and Jeneane Lesko, but by 1957 interest in the barnstorming teams had waned. Major league ball players had returned from war, television brought games into the homes of Americans, and as the country returned to a stricter definition of femininity, there was little interest in seeing women play baseball. Allington and his players could not make enough money to sustain the touring, so in spring 1958 the Allington All-Stars played their last game. Former AAGPBL players who toured with Allington remember it as a tough but rewarding time. Jeneane DesCombes Lesko spoke to the significance of those extra years of professional baseball in a poem:

> We stick together not for money alone
> For we can all get jobs if we return home.
> But, we love the game and deep down inside
> There's a glowing warmth and a heartfelt pride.
>
> There may be no trophy for winning the game
> But the pressure's there just the same.
> We must make the catch or hit the long drive
> For these are the things on which we thrive.
>
> So we'll travel around from pillar to post,
> Go without sleep and live on toast.
> For our love of the game we'll give our best,
> After the season, then we'll rest.[7]

After Allington's barnstorming teams disbanded, the opportunity for organized play diminished. Most former AAGPBL players went on with their lives, starting families and launching careers. But many continued to play casually, and they never forgot how important it was to have the opportunity to play professionally. Some of the players hoped that one day there would be another women's league, and that women would again have the chance to play the game they loved at a high level.

It would be forty years before there was another women's professional baseball team. In the meantime, new generations of young women participated in amateur women's baseball leagues in nearly every region of the country. In New England and Chicago, in Florida and Michigan, and in Washington, D.C., and California, women gathered on baseball diamonds for amateur play. There was no money to pay the players, and the facilities were unkempt and treacherous. But the chance to play far outweighed the difficulties of playing in such venues. Interest among fans was minimal, and there was no media coverage for the games. As a result, much of this history has been lost. Anecdotal evidence suggests, however, that amateur play for women grew in the years following the shuttering of the AAGPBL.

Women also umpired, albeit occasionally. As difficult as it was for women to find opportunities to play baseball, it was even harder for them to break into authority or leadership positions. The patriarchal hierarchy of the game helps to explain the dearth of female umpires. In Jean Ardell's characterization, "If baseball is our national religion and ballparks our green cathedrals, the umpire serves as a parish priest." Umpires were seen as authority figures on the field, and thus the job was not viewed as appropriate for women. During the twelve years of the All-American Girls Professional Baseball League there were no female umpires. It was one thing to allow women to play the game, particularly during

Photographer and associate member of the AAGPBL-PA Cami J. Kidder (left) with Mary Moore (right), suited up and ready to play (photograph by Cami J. Kidder).

the wartime emergency, but another thing entirely to let them control the game. Through most of the twentieth century, even games played by women were umpired by men. And despite a few attempts by women to break into umpiring, even today few women umpire at the minor or major league level.

With the same tenacity that girls and women displayed when attempting to carve out places in which to play baseball, however, some women created umpiring opportunities for themselves. While none of the AAGPBL players ever moved behind the plate in any kind of official way, the league did inspire some women to become umpires. Lefty Alvarez, for example, played softball on local teams in Fort Wayne, Indiana, in the late 1950s. Once people knew that she had played for the AAGPBL, they started telling her about what the league had meant to them—how they, too, dreamed of playing baseball. "This one woman," Lefty said, "started telling me how much she loved baseball but could never play because her mother wouldn't let her play a boy's game so she never learned the game as a kid. Then she saw us in our last season, and even though she wasn't a very good player, she started learning how to umpire games for kids."[8] Because this woman saw other women playing the game she loved, she was able to create a place for herself.

When girls see other girls and women on the field, doing things they did not know women could do, it plants a seed for things to come, allowing them to dream. Some dreamed of umpiring. Others continued to fight for the right to play. Fortunately for both groups, the women's movement arrived just when they needed it. By the late 1960s, the

Grace DeVinney, age 12. A member of Girls Travel Baseball and, as Maybelle Blair herself says, "one of Blair's girls" (photograph by Tammy Adams).

6. *The Next Generation*

National Organization for Women's call for equal access to jobs and education was already making an impact. Women were breaking into formerly male-defined preserves, and this included leadership in baseball. In 1969, Bernice Gera became the first professional female umpire of a minor league baseball game. Formerly a secretary, Gera had decided to change professions when she was in her thirties. After selling her husband on the idea, she entered the Florida Baseball School in 1967 and began training to be an umpire. Since the school had no facilities for women, she lived in a hotel for the six weeks of the program. Although Gera excelled, the National Association of Baseball Leagues (NABL) refused to place her, claiming that she did not meet the physical requirements to be a professional umpire. Gera took the NABL to court, and in 1972 she won a discrimination suit. She worked her first professional game on June 24, 1972. The stress of the fight took its toll on Gera's health, shortening her career, but the precedent was set.[9]

In the 1970s, the impact of the women's movement, and especially the passage of Title IX, gave girls and women new hope for full participation in baseball. Little League, the only available option for most kids who wanted to play ball, became the focus of attention. Maybelle Blair remembers, "I used to take my nephew to his games and I never saw any girls playing. I always looked for them."[10] When Blair was attending Little League games, only boys were allowed to play, but that began to change after the passage of Title IX in 1972. It would, however, take several lawsuits before girls were allowed on Little League fields.

During the summer of 1973, Little League denied a nine-year-old girl from Pawtucket, Rhode Island, named Alison "Pookie" Fortin the opportunity to play Little League baseball. Fortin's family took the league to court, but, impatient with the lengthy legal process, they decided to drop the case. Instead, a number of parents established a separate girls' baseball league, which they initially called the Darlington Pioneer League, and then the Slaterettes. League president Don Phanuef recently explained why the league matters.

> The league has always been there to make sure girls have a place to come every year and play baseball. When girls play with boys, they are sometimes subjected to taunting and made to feel inferior. Kids do that when they are young. With our League, the girls can participate without the pressure of competition. There's more camaraderie involved.

125

The Slaterettes league has continued to grow, and today, according to Phanuef, 165 girls play baseball with the league each year.[11]

Much like the All-American Girls Professional Baseball League did in the 1940s and 1950s, the Slaterettes provided an opportunity for girls to play baseball with each other without the added pressure of competing with boys. But for most girls, fighting their way into Little League was the only available option. In 1974, Janine Cinseruli, from Peabody, Massachusetts, filed a lawsuit against Little League, beginning a wave of resistance against the ban on girls' play. Over the next couple of years, another twenty girls from around the country filed suits arguing their right to play baseball in Little League facilities. The Little League organization spent nearly $2 million to keep girls from playing. Arguing that girls had an equal chance to play ball in their softball leagues, Little League appealed every lower court ruling against it. But when the Appellate Division of the New Jersey Supreme Court ruled that girls had the right to play, Little League had only two choices: take the case to the Supreme Court or stop its fight. The organization ended the struggle to keep girls out of the game in 1974. That summer, nine-year-old Elizabeth Osder took the field in Englewood, New Jersey, becoming the first girl to play Little League baseball under the Supreme Court ruling.[12]

Maybelle Blair was unaware of the lawsuits against Little League or the legal changes they made for young girls. But she definitely remembers the outcome from her many trips to Little League games with her nephew. "Then one day," she remembers, "I looked up and there were girls on the field. Not many, but some, and I thought, 'Well, where have you been? It is about time.'" Every single one of those girls made her proud. "Few of the girls from those early days of Little League knew about us. We didn't talk about it much then—the league, I mean. But I was proud because I knew how important it was for them to play. It also made me a little sad," she admitted. "A lot of years were wasted not letting girls play; just think where we would be today if after our league ended someone would have just picked it up and started another league."[13] Blair expresses very well the frustrations that linger despite the many gains.

After a long fight and numerous lawsuits, girls do play, and the numbers increase every year. Little League estimates the number of girls currently participating in its programs to be about 100,000, and nearly five million girls have played Little League baseball and softball in the past 30 years.[14] However, the fact that Little League, Inc., combines many of the statistics for girls playing baseball with the numbers for softball is an indication that, even today, it is hard for the organization to give girls an equal shot at baseball. There are few opportunities for girls in baseball once they hit their early teens, and even in Little League, rather than foster their growth as baseball players, teenage girls are encouraged to play softball. For boys, Little League is their beginning, a place to learn the sport and hone their skills. For girls, it is more often the beginning and the end of baseball.

In the 1980s, the absence of a feeder system made it doubly hard for women's baseball to grow. But, as was true at every stage of women's baseball history, women fought hard for the opportunity to play the game they loved. Women continued to play on amateur teams around the country. And during that decade there were a couple of notable attempts to create professional teams for women. Perhaps the best known of these teams was founded by Bob Hope, a former Atlanta Braves executive and the owner of an Atlanta public relations firm. In 1984, Hope tried to field a women's minor league team called the Sun Sox. He negotiated with the Class-A Florida State League and believed he had secured a spot for the team. With that in mind, Hope held tryouts for the team, but it quickly became clear that few women had the skill to compete at the required level. Eventually, he compromised, creating a team of both men and women, but he was not able to secure a franchise in the Florida State League as he had hoped.

While Hope was trying to get women into the men's game, others around the country were creating separate amateur women's leagues. These leagues would strive to create a platform on which girls' and women's baseball could grow around the country. The first was the American Women's Baseball Association (AWBA), founded in Chicago in 1988. Created by Darlene Mehrer, the league was the first all-women's league since the AAGPBL. Mehrer successfully fielded women's teams in the Chicago area, and even though she was unable to expand the league nationally, her work was noticed by many around the country who also sought to put women on a baseball diamond. Among others, Jim Glennie of Lansing, Michigan, heard about what Mehrer was doing. At the time, he was coaching his daughter's Little League team. Glennie reached out to Mehrer, and in their first conversation she gave him a history lesson. She told him about the AAGPBL and the importance of that league to the history of girls and women in baseball—and to its future. Glennie took that lesson to heart and used the story of the AAGPBL as publicity when he created the American Women's Baseball Federation in 1992. Like Mehrer, Glennie was dedicated to women's baseball, even paying for uniforms and travel expenses out of his own pocket.[15]

The 1980s saw growth for women in umpiring as well. Only a few years after Bernice Gera's debut, Pam Postema was hired to umpire in the Rookie Gulf Coast League in Florida. She spent a total of thirteen seasons in the minor leagues, eventually moving up to the Triple-A Pacific Coast League in 1983. Postema left the game in 1989, and soon after that another generation of young women tried to break into umpiring. While none of these women ever umpired for the major leagues, some were able to secure positions in Double-A leagues such as the Southern League, and others found jobs in the Independent Pioneer League. A few female umpires made a living from calling baseball games, but a larger number volunteered simply to be part of baseball.

In the 1990s, the release of the movie *A League of Their Own* reshaped America's relationship with girls' and women's baseball. In watching the movie, many Americans saw for the first time women playing baseball in an organized professional league. One point of the film was that the AAGPBL players were in fact skilled athletes. For the many women already playing, the movie became a source of pride and an important connection to their baseball past. For others, it inspired new interest in women's baseball. Although it is impossible to know exactly how the film influenced this trend, the number of girls who joined local Little League teams grew after the movie's debut.[16] More directly, the film became the catalyst that led to the creation of the first professional women's baseball team since the AAGPBL.

The story of the Silver Bullets begins with Bob Hope, who did not give up on his dream of creating a women's baseball team after being turned down by the minor leagues. In 1993, Hope was able to build on the popularity of *A League of Their Own* to convince the Coors Brewing Company to sponsor an all-female baseball club. The film allowed Hope to show Coors, and the country, that women's baseball was not only possible but also exciting, fun and marketable. He secured over $2 million in sponsorship from Coors.

Hope then convinced baseball great Phil Niekro to manage the Silver Bullets.[17] They held invitation-only tryouts at Tinker Field in Orlando, Florida, on December 18, 1993. Twenty-two players were chosen for intensive workouts that lasted for a week. Then, in January and February, the Silver Bullets began a series of open tryouts across the country. Joe Niekro ran the tryouts along with the Orlando Cubs manager and former major leaguer Tommy Jones. The tryout camps were held in Orlando, Knoxville, Atlanta, Chicago, New York, Houston, Sacramento, Mesa, Los Angeles, Denver, and Tacoma. Across the country, nearly 1,300 women attended the tryouts. From these athletes, the Silver Bullets invited fifty-five women to attend spring training.[18]

In a scene that echoed the arrival of the All-American Girls

Former players warming up before an exhibition in Houston, Texas, 2006.

The All-American Girls After the AAGPBL

Professional Baseball League players at their spring tryout in May 1943, forty-nine women descended on Tinker Field in Orlando on Saturday, March 5, 1994. Teachers, coaches, students, mothers, waitresses, and attorneys all put their lives on hold for a chance to play professional baseball with the Colorado Silver Bullets.[19]Like the women of the AAGPBL, most of the athletes who tried out for the Silver Bullets were former college softball players. But two were already well known in the world of baseball. Gina Satriano had played baseball in California, where she worked as a deputy district attorney; when she learned of the chance to try out for the Silver Bullets, she took a leave of absence from her job. Julie Croteau had gone to court to force her Virginia high school to allow her to play. Although she lost that case, she later became the first woman to play, and eventually coach, baseball at the college level.[20] Croteau played first base for the Division III St. Mary's College and later coached baseball at Western New England College. She, too, dropped everything to go play for the new professional team.

The Colorado Silver Bullets barnstormed around the country playing men's amateur and semi-pro teams. In the three and a half months of its first season, the team traveled more than twenty-five thousand miles across the United States and Canada, ending the season with a 6–38 record.[21] The team struggled through losing seasons for three years. In the fourth season, the players posted a winning record of 23–22, but that would be their last season. After four years, the Coors Brewing Company decided not to continue its sponsorship. But even though the team itself was short lived, its impact is illustrated by the success of former Silver Bullet players. After the 1994 season, Lee Anne Ketcham and Julie Croteau both signed with the Class A and AA men's Hawaii Winter Baseball League. They were the first women to play baseball at that level. In 1996, Pam Davis, in a guest appearance with the AA Jacksonville Suns, pitched a scoreless inning of relief against the Australian Olympic men's team.

Individually and as a team, the Silver Bullets broke a lot of new ground, and for that reason they were recognized by the National Baseball Hall of Fame in Cooperstown. The team brought women's baseball to the forefront for the four years of its existence, and it gave many hope that another women's professional league would someday exist. Some of the former AAGPBL players, like Maybelle Blair, saw the creation of the Silver Bullets as a good start in developing women's baseball:

> It had been 40 years since our league ended, and even though most of us didn't talk about it a lot, we hoped there would be another league. I'm not taking credit for those girls, and all of them are better than I ever was, but I do think we had just a little to do with making it OK for them to play in the 1990s.[22]

Maybelle makes an excellent point. Because American baseball fans saw what the AAGPBL did in the 1940s and 1950s, it was easier to envision another women's team. The opposite is also true: when the Silver Bullets folded, it created a vacuum for women's baseball. As Maybelle put it, "The problem is that without a team or league like this one [the Silver Bullets], we are invisible. Women play baseball all the time, but without [television] coverage people just don't know it."[23]

Despite the continued media disinterest, women's amateur play became more organized in the 1990s. Jim Glennie spent much of the decade promoting women's baseball and seeking sponsorships for his teams.[24] The Women's National Adult Baseball Association (WNABA) was formed in 1994. By 1995, the WNABA had affiliated a hundred women's teams located in sixteen states around the country. But not every venture was successful. In 1997, San Diego businessman Mike Ribant formed the Ladies League Baseball. After a season, they expanded to six teams, going nationwide, but lack of attendance forced them to fold shortly thereafter.[25] Also, by 1999, Jim Glennie was exhausted and ready to step back from the movement. However, while there many ups and downs for women's baseball, players and organizers kept trying.

After decades of struggle, the early years of the twenty-first century finally brought sustained growth to women's baseball. In part, this had to do with the connections American teams made with the growing international women's baseball scene. In 2000, a specially selected team flew to Japan to play Team Energen, the Japanese women's national team. The next year, the first Women's World Series was played at the SkyDome in Toronto. The United States, Australia, Canada, and Japan competed, and, in its first international competition, the U.S. team won the gold medal. Meanwhile, on the domestic front, Jim Glennie's group, the American Women's Baseball Federation (AWBF), in 2003 produced the first women's baseball team to be sanctioned by USA Baseball. That same year, women's baseball became an official sport of the Amateur Athletic Union (AAU).

The story of how that happened has everything to do with Justine Siegal, a woman with a long baseball history. In addition to coaching youth baseball, Siegal was one of the first women to coach in collegiate baseball. She was an assistant baseball coach at Springfield College. In 2009, Siegal became the first female coach of a professional men's baseball team when she worked for the Brockton Rox as the first-base coach. In 2011, at the age of 36, she was the first woman to throw batting practice to an MLB team, the Cleveland Indians, during spring training, and she was hired by the Oakland Athletics in 2015 for a two-week coaching stint in their instructional league, becoming the first female coach of a major league baseball team.

Siegal was also active in women's baseball—among other achievements, she formed the Women's Baseball League, Inc. In 1999, she started an electronic newsletter that was crucial to reaching interested players and helping spread the word about opportunities in girls' and women's baseball. And in 2002, Siegal began talks with the Amateur Athletic Union (AAU). The AAU is dedicated to the promotion and development of amateur sports and physical fitness programs. Since its founding in 1888, it has focused on creating common standards in amateur sports and has grown over the years to become one of the leading and most influential associations in the sports world. In a major victory for women's baseball, Siegal convinced the AAU to accept girls' and women's baseball as official AAU sports.[26] For the first time in U.S. history, a national organization sanctioned and supported women's baseball.

Despite all of the growth of the 1990s and early 2000s, none of the leagues founded during these years were able to establish a national movement or organization that could unite the smaller independent groups. Male-dominated baseball organizations continued to resist giving financial support to women's baseball. Because of that lack of cohesion and support, women still had difficulty finding playing opportunities in the United States.

Although women who wanted to play baseball on leagues and teams of their own struggled to realize their goals, opportunities for

Mary Lou Hamilton teeing off. They really never stop (photograph by Cami J. Kidder).

girls to play baseball grew in the 2000s. While many individuals contributed to the growth of girls' baseball, Justine Siegal has once again been especially important and visible, helping to launch a movement. Siegal has a long history of coaching girls. In 2002, she put together an all-girls team called the Sparks, which competed in a national baseball tournament that was otherwise made up entirely of boys' teams. And, believing that girls needed a national organization to advocate for them, she founded (and today still directs) Baseball for All, an organization that works to create opportunities for girls to play baseball.

Justine Siegal is very aware that the women of the All-American Girls Professional Baseball League made it possible for her, and the girls she now mentors, to play the game. In 2015 Baseball for All hosted the first girls' national baseball tournament in Orlando, Florida. The clinics that preceded the games, as well as the opening and closing ceremonies, featured AAGPBL players Maybelle Blair and Shirley Burkovich. Siegal's invitation to the women was a recognition of their role in getting girls on the baseball diamond. To the girls themselves, Maybelle and Shirley were superstars. No matter where the former AAGPBL players were during the tournament, young girls surrounded them. They wanted pictures and autographs and, as Maybelle said, "I think they just wanted to be with us. Maybe they couldn't believe how old we were," she added with a laugh. "Seriously, though, it was like they just couldn't believe we were sitting there."[27] Despite the eighty-year difference in age, those young girls wanted the same thing the AAGPBL players had wanted—to play baseball. And even to those children, the role that the All-American Girls Professional Baseball League had played in making that happen was clear.

At the closing ceremonies Maybelle and Shirley were asked to lead the teams and fans in singing the AAGPBL song. The song was made popular in *A League of Their Own*, so they generally expect some people to know a few of the words. Reluctantly, they picked up the microphone and started singing. Within seconds, the crowd took over. "Wow. They knew the song, all of it, every word," Shirley commented. "That's amazing."[28] It was amazing, but it was also an indication of what coaches and organizers of girls' and women's baseball recognize—that the women of the All-American Girls Professional Baseball League helped start the growth in women's baseball by playing the game, and, perhaps even more significant, they have fostered its growth in the years since the league ended.

For many girls and women who play baseball, along with parents, coaches, sponsors, organizers and fans, knowing that women's baseball has a history is important because they feel the power of having a past. Karen and Josh DeVinney have coached and organized girls' baseball for years. Both of their children, Grace and Will, play baseball. In fact, Grace participated in the inaugural Baseball for All tournament. Recently, I asked the DeVinneys about the importance of knowing and acknowledging the history of women's baseball. Grace responded more eloquently than one might expect from a twelve-year-old, demonstrating the power of the thread that runs through multiple generations. "Knowing Ms. Maybelle personally and that she has opened up opportunities for me in future years to continue to play baseball gives me the power to keep on trying," she wrote. "It gives me the chance to live a part of her legacy."[29] Grace has a very mature understanding and appreciation for the women who came before her. This is not surprising, given her parents' response:

134

6. The Next Generation

The importance of knowing history, to see where you have come and to see where you are going, is an invaluable gift. Being a parent to two athletic children that have both chosen to play baseball is exciting and challenging. The excitement is especially poignant with our oldest child, Grace, who has a deep passion for baseball. Girls historically have not been given the same opportunities as their male counterparts over the last several decades, as unjust as that is. There is no greater divide than to witness your daughter trying to make her way through the sport of baseball. Grace has only been playing since she was eight and in these four short years has had some of the most incredible experiences, both positive and negative. The greatest gift we can give our children is to expose them to situations and opportunities that enable growth. Grace has been blessed with not only getting to meet historical pioneers like Maybelle Blair and Shirley Burkovich but to have formed a genuine friendship with Maybelle. It's truly like the pages of history have come to life and my daughter has been granted a gift to not only learn what a powerful role these two women have played in the sport of baseball, but the powerful role they have played in fighting for equality of women. Because of their fight, their tenacity and their drive, Grace has the opportunity to play a sport she loves just as much as Maybelle and Shirley [did].[30]

Those experiences have also meant a lot to Maybelle and Shirley themselves, as they have been granted an opportunity to see their legacy played out.

The DeVinneys are one element of a huge force of women and men who work to make girls' baseball a reality around the country. Justine Siegal, as mentioned previously, is the founder of Baseball for All; John Kovach, a baseball coach in Chicago, founded the United States Girls Baseball Association; Mary Jo Stegeman leads the Chicago Pioneers Girls Baseball team; Deb Bettencourt is the administrator of the Pawtucket Slaterettes; and Robert Saven and Josh DeVinney cofounded Girls Travel Baseball (GTB). These are only a few of the individuals around the country today who put girls on the field and keep the ties between the past and the future of girls' baseball strong. As the DeVinneys explain,

Grace has been granted the opportunity to play with an elite group of female baseball athletes. She continues to have the chance to play with exceptional girls from all across this country with her Girls Travel Baseball team. This team was formed by some parents that wanted to give their daughters a chance to play baseball more regularly in tournaments in the United States. It is the hope that this GTB Elite Team can continue to bring awareness and show just how much girls love baseball and that they have the athletic talent to hang with their male counterparts. It's with sincere gratitude and respect for the trail blazers like Maybelle Blair and Shirley Burkovich that these girls, any girls should never let their love of baseball be diminished because they are girls.[31]

It now seems possible that, decades later, we are finally poised to realize the dream of the AAGPBL players: a world where no one questions whether girls can or should play baseball.

In the introduction of her thesis "Stealing Home: Why Baseball Isn't America's National Pastime," Emma Charlesworth-Seiler compares the difficult journey of girls and women who want to play baseball in the United States with the "riskiest play in baseball, stealing home." Stealing home, she explains, "takes guts and guile, courage and tenacity." For girls who are often the only female on a Little League or high school team, it takes courage to refuse the "softball line"—to stand up to the societal pressure that says boys play baseball, while girls play softball. A female baseball player must know all of her options and be prepared to take the consequences. To successfully steal home,

> The baserunner must have an exceptional understanding of the situation: score, inning, number of outs, who else is on base, the skills of the batter, the count on the batter, the routine of the pitcher, how quickly the pitcher commits to pitch, the tendencies of the catcher, where the infielders are playing, what plays the third base coach is running, and what the weather and field conditions are like.

Even if a player is able to do all these things in a split second, few baserunners attempt to steal home. It is rarely successful, and they risk personal injury from being hit by the ball or the bat. "For women who endeavor to play baseball," Charlesworth-Seiler concludes, "their journey is much like stealing home."[32]

For many girls and women today, getting on the field at all is a bit like trying to steal home, but they keep trying. Some girls, like Mo'ne Davis and Kendra Levesque, have been successful at making their mark in the game of baseball. Mo'ne Davis led her team to the Little League World Series in 2014, and she became the first girl to throw a shutout in the history of the event. Her appearance on the cover of *Sports Illustrated* sealed her fame. That same year, Kendra Levesque became the first girl to win the King of Swat home-run hitting contest at Cooperstown Dreams Park. Beating out more than 100 boys, she was hailed as the Queen of Swat. Davis and Levesque are exceptions that represent what is possible if girls are given the chance to play.

6. *The Next Generation*

Although America claims baseball as its national pastime, ironically women's baseball is much bigger internationally than it is in this country. Because of this, today the best opportunities for women to play are on U.S. teams that compete internationally. Since 2004, USA Baseball has sponsored the Women's National Team, participating that year in the first international women's baseball tournament. Every two years there is a series of regional tryouts, and those selected are invited to the National Training Complex in North Carolina. From that group, twenty women are chosen to play on the U.S. national team.

Left to right: **Kendra Levesque and Maybelle Blair. A member of the organization Baseball for All, Kendra represents the large number of girls who play baseball today. In 2014, Kendra became the first girl to win the King of Swat competition in Cooperstown, New York, beating out 103 boys and earning the title of "Queen of Swat." Her hat is on display at the National Baseball Hall of Fame.**

In the summer of 2008, Marti Sementelli thought she was walking into a scene from a new *A League of Their Own* when she stepped out onto the field at the USA Women's Baseball tryouts. Although more than a hundred women tried out for the team that year, "I didn't even know there were others girls who played baseball," Sementelli said. "They were all just like me," she realized. "I was like, 'Woah!' I was shell-shocked because I had so much in common with them." The event was overwhelming. "I really thought

137

I was dreaming. It didn't look real."[33] It was very real, however, and Sementelli made the team.

The members of the Women's National Team train together and are then sent to the Women's World Cup. In 2004, the inaugural Women's Baseball World Cup was held in Canada. From that first international competition, women's international baseball has grown significantly. Although not all countries compete in the World Cup, there are many that have strong women's teams, including Australia, Canada, Chinese Taipei, South Korea, Hong Kong, India, Japan, Venezuela, Puerto Rico, the Netherlands, Cuba, Israel, and Vietnam. Unlike in the United States, the international teams and the leagues have strong financial support. This support allows for more growth and training for young girls who want to play baseball, a very effective way of increasing opportunities. Girls have the chance to play from an early age and a number of options as they get older. By the time they are old enough to play for their national team, they have been playing for a number of years.[34]

Despite the relative lack of opportunity, however, American women continue to play baseball. In 2015, the U.S. national team won the first gold medal awarded for women's baseball at the Pan Am Games. They got no money and very little media attention. In fact, despite the success at the Pan Am Games, few Americans even know there is a national team. International baseball does not hold the same interest for Americans that it does elsewhere. Most American baseball fans believe that the best baseball is played in the United States, and that international leagues are simply not as good. This attitude makes it even easier to ignore the accomplishments of the U.S. women's national team. Many people believe that if women aren't playing in the United States and winning at a high level of play, then they must not be playing at all. But they *are* playing—and winning. Women seek opportunities internationally because so few exist in the United States. All they want is to play. They do it because they love the game.

"The chance to play baseball was just dropped in our laps," Maybelle Blair said. "We didn't have to fight to get out there like the girls do today. Our battle was not in getting there but staying there. I wish we could have kept it going. For us and for them."[35] But while it may not seem like girls' and women' baseball has been growing, in reality it has been developing slowly but consistently over the past seventy-plus years. Unusual circumstances, wartime, Depression-era travel restrictions and a desire to keep the game alive made it possible for women to play professional baseball in the 1940s and 1950s. Even though it appeared as if women stopped playing the game in 1954 when the league ended, clearly that was not the case. Women who were dedicated to baseball created amateur leagues for themselves; they fought for girls to play Little League, to play on high school and college baseball teams. Women worked as umpires and coaches, even community organizers, just so that girls and women would have the opportunity to play baseball. A whole movement emerged around creating opportunities for girls and women in baseball, and today there are more chances for girls to play and for women to coach and umpire. Equality in the game is still a long way off, but when it is possible to chart the growth from one generation to the next, when an unbroken tie remains in place for over 70 years, there is hope.

Literally hundreds of girls' and women's teams and leagues exist just in North America. If a girl wants to play baseball, she will have to look, but the opportunities are out there. It is difficult to trace a straight line of progress between the All-American Girls Professional Baseball League of the 1940s and 1950s and the girls who play baseball today. Instead, progress has taken many turns. It has stalled at times and flashed forward at others. But one constant has been the connection that exists between the pioneers of the past and the pioneers of the future. "We don't know how this will all end up," Maybelle Blair said of the movement to create women's baseball in the United States, "but if I have my way, from here on out girls will play baseball when and where they want to and hopefully when they are done playing they will enjoy their success, then put out a hand and help the next girl coming down the pike. That's what we did, still do."[36]

Conclusion

"Sports. It's your heart. It's your soul. It's who you are. It's your gift. You may not know it, but we, you, all of us are all better when you share it."

—Ron Webb[1]

It is possible to read this entire book as a story about a group of women who held well-paying jobs at a time when most women did not, experienced exceptional educational and career success, and then became famous. But that would miss the point. As Delores "Dolly" Brumfield White explained, "That [All-American Girls Professional Baseball League] salary made a huge difference in the lives of so many people. But you know what made it sweeter, the fact that we earned it on a baseball field."[2] Those jobs and that fame came about because these women played *baseball*. And baseball was never just a game to them; it was stronger than that. Janet "Pee Wee" Wiley (1950–1953) remembered the moment when she was first offered a contract to play professional baseball:

I got a call and was told that the South Bend Blue Sox has chosen me, and I was offered a contract. I was so happy I thought someone would pinch me, and I would find out it was a dream. It was a dream all right, but one that came true.[3]

Baseball mattered because it was and is the heart of who these women were and are. It helped to define them.

The women of the AAGPBL were in many ways a diverse group. They came from rural areas of the Midwest, urban sections of the northeast, and farming communities of the South. They were Californians, Canadians and Cubans. The league drew its members from different classes and from different ages and levels of talent. And it had

The latest group photograph of the AAGPBL players. South Bend, Indiana, 2015 (photograph by Kaitlyn Haines).

some racial and ethnic diversity (limited by the exclusion of African Americans). All of these different aspects of identity went into making up who these women were. None of this, however, gives us an image of the members of the AAGPBL that they themselves would recognize, because it fails to include baseball.

What does it mean to think of baseball as a fundamental part of who someone is? That baseball, or sports more generally, are central to a person's sense of self? I call this concept *sport identity*.[4] For a person who is sport identified, their sense of who they are as an athlete is as important as their race, class or gender. This is a simple concept, but it can be a powerful one. When I explain this idea, I often only get as far as naming it before women start to tell me that they are sport identified, as though they were just waiting for the concept to come along. Sport identity gives a name to an important facet of themselves, something they knew existed but couldn't identify, that was bigger than "I played sports." Sport identity can also be valuable as a tool for historians. It allows us to understand both why the AAGPBL players felt they

Conclusion

had rediscovered their family when they first reunited in the 1980s and why this particular group of women forces us to think differently about history.

For sport-identified women, the experience of playing sports is often at the heart of their sense of self-confidence and mastery in the world. It is what they feel at the core of their strength; in fact, it provides that strength. This comes across over and over again in the stories of the league's women. Before Maddy English joined the league, she was shy and insecure.

> I was the quiet one who didn't talk much and I was not able to speak in front of groups at all. My experiences in the league not only helped me pay for college, but also gave me confidence in myself. I became a teacher, teaching physical education, English literature, and early American history. I was no longer fearful about speaking in front of people. I believed in myself, and felt I could achieve my goal of helping students.

Former AAGPBL player Shirley Burkovich coaching the newest generation of girls who play baseball (photograph by Debbie Pierson).

142

Conclusion

For Maddy, the confidence that playing gave her made everything else possible. "There is no telling where I'd be," she explained. "Without it [baseball] I would not have had the confidence to attend college, coach or become a counselor."[5] Echoing Maddy's message, Jacqueline "Jackie" Mattson (1950–1951) said,

> In many situations, I have been a winner. But it is important that you learn how to lose, like when I was with the Kenosha Comets and they folded. One cannot always be a winner. This is what builds character.[6]

The security, confidence and ability to cope with life's challenges that sports provide remained with the league players throughout their lives.

Former AAGPBL player Maybelle Blair at the Girls National Baseball Tournament, Orlando, Florida, in May 2015 (author's photograph).

Conclusion

For some of the women, the sense of self that baseball provided went deeper. It didn't just give them opportunities for growth and in life but also rescued them. As Lefty claimed, "It was my life in sports, my connections to sports, that saved me. Holy cow, where would I have been? Where would I be without it?"[7] Maybelle Blair echoes the idea that sports can serve as a lifelong anchor:

> I used sports, my understanding of it and my connection to it, my whole life. As a manager of the transportation division at Northrup Airlines I always asked potential drivers if they had played sports. If they had, I knew they would be good drivers because they were good in their bodies. That's who I hired. I know because I know it for myself. Sports help to make you.[8]

Here Maybelle suggests another aspect of sport identity: like other forms of identity, sport identity is shaped by the belief that it is rooted in the body. Many players have spoken of their conviction that some people have a natural affinity for sports—that some women are born to play. Whether it is something a woman is born to do or something that comes through training, sport identity is an embodied identity.

For some league women, baseball also provided a sense of connection and shared meaning. Sport identity doesn't happen in a vacuum; rather, it is shaped by the culture that structures it. While playing in the league the women shared profound and life-altering experiences. In the period between the league's ending in 1954 and the first reunion, the players' contributions to baseball and the war effort were erased. The experience of everyone denying their history as players led to an even stronger bond between them. They spent years trying to explain their past as baseball players and were often met with shrugs or disbelief. When they finally reconnected in the 1980s, the sense of oneness and relief, and the comfort of being with those who shared that history, felt like coming home. Sports, as well as the shared experiences and culture, helped to define the women of the AAGPBL, and it was sports that gave them the opportunity to simply pick up where they left off when their playing days ended.

Finally, while sport identity theory doesn't claim that sports are more important than other forms of identification, they can be the heart of the matrix, the piece that allows women to make sense of all the various aspects of who they are. Lefty Alvarez is a particularly good example of this concept. She rarely identifies herself as only Cuban, or as working class, or as a woman. Instead, she nearly always refers to herself as a female, Cuban American baseball player. "Baseball player" always comes last—it is where she ends the phrase, the location of emphasis. For women like Lefty, sports are where all other identity markers merge to create self-expression and self-awareness.

Sport identity helps to explain why their few years of playing baseball were so transformative for the AAGPBL players. For sport-identified women, sports are at the center of their sense of power in the world; it is where they find a sense of belonging, a shared identity. It is the connective tissue that holds the sport-identified woman together and the thing that many feel they were born to do. Sport identity clarifies why these women are who they are, and why getting to play in the AAGPBL wasn't, for most of them, just a cool thing they did for a few summers—and why they have rewritten history.

My students' challenge to me to prove my claim about the importance of women's access to sports is what originally led me to the women of the AAGPBL. And in every women's history class I have taught since, I have told my students about the discussion that started it all. I share with them the historical evidence I uncovered at the urging of their predecessors, empowering them through the example of how my former students were part of my quest for historical proof. And then I tell them the story.

The story of the AAGPBL and its players provides a window into the role that sports can play in the lives of women. We see, through their stories, how playing professional baseball changed their lives in very profound ways. They were able to earn larger salaries than most women of the time, which gave them unprecedented independence and opened up career opportunities. They traveled and experienced political and cultural differences that helped to form them into the broadminded adults they became. Baseball, for them, was a patriotic duty, and their pride in that service encouraged them to remain patriotic and committed to service throughout their lives. They helped to initiate and foster a revolution in women's sports that expanded women's participation, increased the recognition of female athletes, and helped to bring girls' and women's sports to areas of the country where they did not previously exist. Finally, in rediscovering each other and celebrating their shared history, they affirmed the centrality of sports in their lives.

I still have students who shrug their shoulders, roll their eyes and proclaim, "But it's only baseball." But, I tell them, baseball is never "just a game." Having access to baseball can be more than merely a chance to play. For me, it was a lifeline. I was a poor kid who was also labeled a "slow learner," and in elementary school I had virtually no confidence in myself. I was shy and had never been separated from my mother before, so starting first grade nearly killed me. I struggled to read as well as the other kids and never seemed to have the right clothes, the right shoes or even the right lunchbox. (Those were the days of metal lunchboxes painted to depict characters from popular television shows. I had *Gunsmoke* when everyone else had *Bonanza*.) This trend did not end as I moved through elementary school, and I quietly endured the loneliness and embarrassment until finally my frustration reached a peak ... over recess.

I did not like the fact that I was expected to play jump rope with the girls while the boys played baseball. After each recess, I sulked and refused to do my work, which did nothing to eliminate my "slow learner" label. When the teacher confronted me, I tried to explain that I was as good a ball player as any of the boys. Even though most of the boys, as well as the teacher, laughed at me, I insisted. My teacher very patiently, and with great sympathy, told me that sports should not matter to a girl, and that if I was better than the boys, I should never let *them* know that! Despite my usual shyness and insecurity in the classroom, I continued to argue and ended up standing in the corner because of it. But the lesson was clear: girls should not like sports, they should not be good at sports, and they certainly should not compare their athletic abilities to those of boys.

What was especially infuriating was that every boy sitting in that classroom had played baseball with me, and when we played in the neighborhood I was often given the task of deciding who played what position and on which team. I don't know exactly how this evolved, but my memory is of little boys standing around me in a circle, waving their hands and asking, "Can I be on your team?" "Can I play first base?" And I thought, "Why are they asking me?" Eventually, I realized that they counted on me because I was a good, confident ball player, a fact they could and did accept on the neighborhood baseball field but openly resisted when confronted with the societal expectations articulated by our teacher. It was very difficult to shift from being accepted, and even admired, to being laughed at and excluded. It would be years before I figured out how to make sense of that contradiction.

Despite all of the social pressure, baseball saved me. On the baseball diamond, I was never the butt of jokes, never the worst performer, never the worst dressed or the dumbest. Instead, I was one of the best— the one with the best arm, the most accurate throw and a voice of authority. My timing was great, and my ability to understand the game and my role in it was extraordinary. In fact, the *only* place I truly felt comfortable, capable, and at home was at short stop. It is no wonder, then, that in every difficult experience of my life, every challenge, regardless of its nature, my body, mind, and emotional state all reverted to the place where I was capable, successful, and a winner. With no conscious effort on my part, I became the person who could and did win ball games, challenging the boys in my neighborhood, and even my teachers.

It was many years before I made a conscious connection between the benefits of baseball and my personal success. It wasn't until I witnessed the same phenomenon at work in the lives of AAGPBL players that I understood. In 2003, when I first met the women of the AAGPBL, first encountered the strong individuals they had become, first heard their stories of challenge and triumph and witnessed the family ties they had forged over 60 years, I realized that it was baseball, access to the game and the tradition, that provided them and me with the foundation on which our lives were built.

Participation in baseball promotes leadership skills and positive body images that enable personal success and healthy lifestyles. It also builds critical life values such as teamwork, self-confidence, and courage. But baseball, as I learned upon meeting the AAGPBL players, is about so much more. It provides a location where girls and women can challenge society's gender constraints. It is a place where girls can be athletic and aggressive. It is a place where girls can win and be proud to be winners. And it gives girls a chance to be included in the traditional narrative of America's favorite pastime. As Lefty says, "I—women like me—are nothing without baseball."[9]

Appendix

Girls' and Women's Baseball

Teams, leagues and organizations that currently promote girls' and women's baseball in the United States and Canada.

United States

CALIFORNIA

Baseball for All—www.baseballforall.com

An advocate group for girls' and women's participation in baseball, Baseball for All was established to foster, educate, empower, and consult on all things related to girls' baseball. Justine Siegal, founder of the organization, has been featured in hundreds of media outlets and has been a trailblazer on behalf of women in the baseball world. In 2015 Baseball for All began holding an annual all-girls national baseball tournament.

International Women's Baseball Center (Cathedral City)— http://www.internationalwomensbaseballcenter.org

With the mantra "Step up to the Sport," the IWBC has set out to protect, preserve, and promote women's baseball. Hosting an annual symposium on girls' and women's baseball and putting together the 2016 Ruth Hartman Memorial Girls Baseball Tournament with the Big Vision Foundation, the IWBC hopes to bring girls' and women's baseball teams and organizations across the country together to strengthen their collective voice.

LA Monarchs (Southern California)—www.lamonarchs.org

This travel team of 9–11-year-old girls was organized to compete in Baseball for All's national tournaments.

Appendix

San Francisco Bay Sox—www.sfbaysoxgirls@gmail.com

Created to compete in the first all-girls national baseball tournament in 2015, the Bay Sox are a team of 10–13-year-old girls. They continue to play in the San Francisco area and are known as Northern California's only all-girls traveling baseball team.

San Francisco Youth Baseball League—www.sfybl.com

After the San Francisco Parks and Recreation sponsored an all-girls team to participate in the Baseball for All Nationals in 2015, the SFYBL has set out to expand its operations to include a girls' league. With Girls Baseball Commissioner Annie Jupiter Jones, the SFYBL hopes to field four all-girls teams in the 2016 season and to continue to provide opportunities for girls to play.

DISTRICT OF COLUMBIA

DC Girls Baseball—http://dcgirlsbaseball.com

Formed to compete in the 2015 national girls tournament, DC Girls Baseball advocates for girls to participate in all sports. This is a travel team that spends the summer traveling nationally for tournaments.

FLORIDA

Girls Travel Baseball—www.girlstravelbaseball.com

GTB strives to recognize individual players, teams, leagues and tournaments that feature girls playing baseball. It also sponsors a travel team to compete in national tournaments.

ILLINOIS

American Eagles—www.ilgirlsbaseball.org/#!eagles/c1fgp

Part of Illinois Girls Baseball, the American Eagles are a 13U team created to compete in Baseball for All's national tournament. The Eagles also compete in tournaments around Illinois and Minnesota.

Chicago Gems Women's Baseball Club— www.chicagogems.com

Featuring three core programs, the CGWBC is dedicated to promoting baseball as a viable mainstream sport for girls and women. For those 14 and older, the club program provides training and recruiting, while its league program has developed into the Chicago Women's Baseball League (CWBL). Utilizing the talent from its league program, every year the CGWBC creates a tournament team, known as the Gems, to play in regional and national tournaments.

Chicago Women's Baseball League—www.chicagowbl.com

An amateur women's baseball league for ages 14–40+, the CWBL is a program of the Chicago Gems Women's Baseball Club.

Rockford Starfires Women's Baseball—www.beyerpark.org

Calling Beyer Stadium, home of the AAGPBL's Rockford Peaches, their home field, the Starfires brought women's baseball back to Rockford in 2012. A women's 18-and-older team, they host the annual Peach Orchard Classic Tournament at Beyer Stadium.

INDIANA

American Women's Baseball Federation (Huntingburg)— www.awbf.org

The AWBF promotes baseball for women as a mainstream sport and lifetime opportunity. It has organized seventeen regional and national tournaments since 1992 and holds a National Championship Tournament in Indiana. Partnering with Japan, the AWBF helped to organize Women's World Series events prior to the creation of the Women's World Cup of Baseball in 2004. Today, the organization maintains a database of players interested in playing for USA Baseball.

MASSACHUSETTS

The BASE (Roxbury)—www.thebase.org

Formed in the 1970s to provide a place for urban youth to have a positive environment, the BASE has served 8,000 boys and girls and sponsored 600 teams throughout its existence. Providing comprehensive athletic and educational advancement opportunities, the organization encourages participants to pursue excellence through sports.

Appendix

Michigan

All-American Girls Professional Baseball League Players Association—www.aagpbl.org

Dedicated to preserving the history of the All-American Girls Professional Baseball League and its players, the AAGPBL Players Association also promotes sports participation through community development. Made up of former players and associate members, the AAGPBL Players Association also has a quarterly newsletter, *Touching Bases*.

Detroit River Belles Ladies Vintage Base Ball Club— www.historicfortwaynecoalition.com

Playing baseball according to the rules and dress from 1869, the River Belles were Michigan's first all-ladies Vintage Base Ball Club. Making their home in Historic Fort Wayne in downtown Detroit, the River Belles compete across the Midwest against ladies' and men's vintage teams.

Lil Fillies Ladies Vintage Base Ball Club (Benton Harbor)— www.facebook.com/TheLilFillies

Founded in August 2013, the Lil Fillies follow the rules and dress of baseball from 1858.

Merries Ladies Vintage Base Ball Club (Chelsea)— www.chelseamonitors.com/merries-home

The Merries are the sister club of Monitor Base Ball Club and play by the 1860s rules and dress of baseball.

Minnesota

Minnesota Girls Baseball Association— www.mngirlsbaseball.org

Encouraging involvement and providing support for girls and women interested in baseball, the Minnesota Girls Baseball Association was founded to challenge the barriers keeping girls and women from playing.

New Jersey

East Coast Yankees Women's Baseball (Basking Ridge)— www.facebook.com/East-Coast-Yankees-Womens-Baseball-121247691286389

Active since 2002, the East Coast Yankees is a women's team that plays in tournaments throughout the United States and Canada.

Pawtucket Slaterettes Baseball League— www.slaterettes.com

The Slaterettes were founded in 1973 after a nine-year-old girl was barred from joining Little League due to her gender. In 2001, 165 girls ranging from ages 5 to 18 were registered to play in the league. Originally meant as a youth league, today the Pawtucket Slaterettes allow girls and women of all ages to play. In 2015, the oldest player was 55.

New Mexico

New Mexico Fusion (Albuquerque)— www.facebook.com/newmexicofusion

Originally created to compete in the Baseball for All tournament, New Mexico Fusion is now a team dedicated to providing life skills through sports to student athletes. The travel team competes in tournaments throughout the country.

New York

New York Women's Baseball Association (New York City)— www.nywomensbaseball.com

With a mission to provide clinics, a summer league, the Bluebirds Baseball League, and the awareness that girls and women play baseball, the New York Women's Baseball Association seeks to provide instruction and competition to girls and women of all skill levels.

North Carolina

USA Baseball (Durham)—www.usabaseball.com

USA Baseball is the organization that selects the U.S. Women's National Baseball Team. Providing players for events like the Pan-Am Games and the Women's World Cup of Baseball, USA Baseball holds an annual Women's National Open to scout potential recruits for national team events and activities.

Pennsylvania

Big Vision Foundation, Inc. (Leesport)— www.bigvisionfoundation.org

Big Vision Foundation is a group dedicated to providing a community atmosphere to the world of baseball. Organizing tournaments throughout the summer, BVF was a partner in putting together the IWBC Ruth Hartman Memorial Girls Baseball Tournament, an all-girls baseball tournament, in June 2016.

Texas

Coastal Baseball Women's League (Houston)— www.coastalbaseball.com

Responding to public demand, the Coastal Baseball League is working to create a women's league within its amateur baseball league. For women 16 and older, the league will support traveling to national tournaments and organize a schedule for women's teams in the area to play one another.

Virginia

Eastern Women's Baseball Conference (Leesburg)— www.ewbc.wordpress.com

Featuring four teams from the DC-Baltimore Metropolitan Area, the EWBC promotes girls' and women's participation in baseball for all ages, skill levels, and locales. This group has provided twenty years of play for women in the area and hosts an annual Memorial Day weekend tournament. The EWBC is also home to DC Thunder, the All-Star team it sponsors for play in regional and national tournaments.

Washington

Puget Sound Senior Baseball League—www.pssbl.com

Founded in 1989 with four teams, the PSSBL has grown to 67 teams, spanning eight age and skill divisions, with more than 1,000 participants.

A pay-to-play league, the PSSBL dropped the gender of its national affiliate, the Men's Senior Baseball League, and includes several women's teams.

Seattle Diamonds Baseball (Bellevue)— www.SeattleDiamondsBaseball.com

The Seattle Diamonds have been a team for the last six years, catering to women in the Seattle and Western Washington area. Part of the Puget Sound Senior Baseball League (PSSBL), they play in the Teton Division against both men's and women's teams. The Diamonds span all ages and skill levels for the senior league (19–70+) and travel to play throughout the United States.

Canada

ALBERTA

Alberta Girls Baseball (Edmonton)— www.albertagirlsbaseball.com

A cooperative effort of Baseball Alberta and Little League Alberta, Alberta Girls Baseball provides sustainable and exceptional programs for female athletes, targeting increased participation and athletic development. Alberta Girls Baseball is open to girls aged 11 or older.

Alberta Women's Midget AA Team (Edmonton and Calgary)—www.albertagirlsbaseball.com/ alberta-women-s-midget-aa-team

The Alberta Women's Midget AA Team is a member of the Baseball Alberta Midget AA League. Intended for girls 15 and older, the team practices in Edmonton and Calgary, but it includes players from across the province.

BRITISH COLUMBIA

Baseball BC (Surrey)—http://baseball.bc.ca

The female program of Baseball BC is designed to provide competition and development in an all-female environment. With four divisions for girls 11 and older, the youth league focuses on skill development. At the end of the summer youth league, Team BC is chosen from among the female teams for the BC Selects Female Baseball Program to compete regionally and nationally.

Manitoba

Baseball Manitoba (Winnipeg)—www.baseballmanitoba.ca

Baseball Manitoba holds open tryouts and play for girls wanting to participate in Manitoba Girls Baseball, a provincial team that represents Manitoba in Baseball Canada's girls' tournaments across the country.

New Brunswick

Baseball New Brunswick (Fredericton)—www.baseballnb.ca

While Baseball New Brunswick does not have a full girls' program, the organization sponsors a Girls' Day each season for girls ages 6–16.

Newfoundland and Labrador

Baseball NL (Paradise)—www.baseballnl.com

Baseball NL sponsors several girls programs, and it has recently expanded to include a director of female baseball in its administration. Sending players to the Girls Evaluation Camp in Cuba and holding a Skills and Drills Identification Camp, Baseball NL is committed to providing opportunities for girls to play at the Pee Wee, Bantam, and Women's levels.

Nova Scotia

Baseball Nova Scotia (Halifax)—
http://baseballnovascotia.com

Baseball Nova Scotia is dedicated to training and developing girls and women to compete in senior women's programs and national programs. The organization holds an eight-week development camp for girls aged 5–10 and a training camp for girls aged 13–21. These girls and women are scouted for provincial and national teams to compete throughout Canada.

ONTARIO

Baseball Canada (Ottawa)—www.baseball.ca

Baseball Canada was incorporated in 1964 as the Canadian Federation of Amateur Baseball. Sponsoring the men's and women's Canadian national teams, Baseball Canada also has ten provincial associations, most of which sponsor girls' baseball programs.

Baseball Milton—www.baseballmilton.com

Affiliated with the Burlington Organized Minor Baseball Association, Baseball Milton provides grassroots-level baseball to build teams to compete in the higher age groups, with the opportunity for girls to participate.

Baseball Ontario (Cambridge)—www.baseballontario.com

Baseball Ontario supports provincial teams at the Bantam, Junior Women's, and Women's levels. Women's teams in the 16-and-older age group can apply to play for Baseball Ontario and compete at the national level for the province.

Burlington Organized Minor Baseball Association— www.baseballburlington.com

BOMBA has had at least one all-girls team since 1991. With a girls' tee-ball league and mixed play with the boys, girl baseball players have the opportunity to play at all levels for BOMBA.

North Toronto Baseball—www.ntbaseball.com

Providing baseball opportunities for 1,200 girls and boys in the North Toronto area, this league has been extremely successful for kids and young adults interested in the sport. Dedicated to balanced teams for more competitive play, the 2016 season opened with almost no remaining spots for teams in the league's seven age divisions.

North York Baseball (Toronto)—www.nyba.ca

Explicitly prohibiting gender discrimination in its league constitution, North York Baseball provides numerous opportunities for girls and boys to participate in baseball. There are no all-girls divisions, but coed play is available.

Appendix

Ontario Women's Baseball League (Toronto)— www.ontariowomensbaseball.com

Formerly the Central Ontario Girls Baseball League, the OWBL caters to both girls and women who want to participate in baseball. A league shaped by its coaches and players, the OWBL supports the Toronto Fusion, a team that plays in international competitions. Both the Fusion and the OWBL provide girls' baseball clinics run by women.

Royal York Baseball (Toronto)—www.rybl.com

With four all-girls divisions and younger coed play, Royal York Baseball is dedicated to providing opportunities for both girls and boys to play.

Toronto Blue Jays—www.toronto.bluejays.mlb.com

The Toronto Blue Jays are committed to Canadian girls' and women's participation in baseball. The organization sponsors the Canadian Women's National Team and hosted four Toronto Blue Jays Baseball Academy Girls Days in 2015 for girls 6–16.

Wexford Agincourt Baseball League (Scarborough)— www.wexfordbaseball.com

Dedicated to providing opportunities for girls and boys to play baseball, the Wexford Agincourt Baseball League offers coed baseball for ages 4–19 and two all-girls divisions (ages 10–13 and 14–16).

SASKATCHEWAN

Saskatchewan Baseball (Regina)—www.saskbaseball.ca

While Sask Baseball does not host a girls' league, it fields all-girls teams for the annual Pee Wee Girls Western Canada Baseball Championship and the Baseball Canada Bantam Girls Championship, providing travel grants to players. To form these teams, Sask Baseball holds training sessions. A provincial championship is held if more than one team in each division is formed.

Saskatoon Royals Baseball— www.saskatoonroyalsbaseball.com

The Saskatoon Royals are a zone in the Saskatoon baseball league. Although they play boys' teams from the other four zones, the Saskatoon Royals provide all-girls teams and competition for girls of all ages, starting in the youngest baseball category at age 4.

Chapter Notes

Introduction

1. Dorothy Seymour Mills and Harold Seymour, *Baseball: The People's Game* (New York: Oxford University Press, 1990), 454.

2. Karen Kunkel helped create the players association throughout the early 1980s and was asked by Penny Marshall to be a consultant for the movie, which premiered in 1992.

3. Susan Cahn, *Coming on Strong: Gender and Sexuality in Twentieth-Century Women's Sport* (Cambridge, MA: Harvard University Press, 1998), 3–4.

4. Steven R. Bullock, *Playing for Their Nation: Baseball and the American Military During World War II* (Lincoln: University of Nebraska Press, 2004), 67.

5. Roosevelt to Landis, January 15, 1942, BA MSS 44, National Baseball Hall of Fame East Archives, Cooperstown, New York.

6. Jeneane Lesko, "League History," Official Website of the AAGPBL: All-American Girls Professional Baseball League Players Association, accessed November 9, 2015, http://aagpbl.org/index.cfm/pages/league/12/league-history.

7. *Ibid.*

8. *Ibid.*

9. Gai Berlage, *Women in Baseball: The Forgotten History* (Westport, CT: Praeger, 1994), 134.

10. Jack Fincher, "The 'Belles of the Game' Were a Hit with Their Fans," *Smithsonian* 20 (1999): 88–97.

11. Lesko, "League History."

12. *Ibid.*

13. Fincher, "The 'Belles of the Game,'" 88–90.

Chapter 1

1. Eleanor Roosevelt, "My Day," December 22, 1945, https://www.gwu.edu/~erpapers/myday/displaydoc.cfm?_y=1945&_f=md000215.

2. Virginia Woolf, *A Room of One's Own* (New York: Harcourt, Brace, 1929), chapter 1.

3. "Pink collar" is a term coined by Louise Kapp Howe to refer to female-majority jobs such as waitress, secretary, beautician, or salesclerk that don't fit comfortably into either the blue-collar or the white-collar categories. Pink-collar jobs are usually low-paying, dead-end positions. See Louise Kapp Howe, *Pink Collar Workers: Inside the World of Women's Work* (New York: G.P Putnam and Sons, 1977), 186–88.

4. Susan Ware, "Women and the Great Depression," Gilder Lehrman Institute of American History, accessed on November 9, 2015, www.gilderlehrman.org/history-by-era/great-depression/essays/women-and-great-depression.

5. Mary Elizabeth Pidgeon, *Changes in Women's Employment during the War*

(Washington, DC: U.S. Department of Labor, Women's Bureau, 1944), 5–6.

6. Judy Barrett Litoff and David Smith, *American Women in a World at War: Contemporary Accounts from World War II*, The Worlds of Women Series (Lanham, MD: Rowman & Littlefield, 1997), 167.

7. For example, when discussing the impact of the war's end on women's employment, most scholars point to national unemployment statistics (which do not include information about athletes) to demonstrate the unfair treatment of female workers after the war. The following books make this omission: Emily Yellin, *Our Mothers' War: American Women at Home and at the Front during World War II* (2004; repr., New York: Free Press, 2005); Ruth Milkman, *Gender at Work: The Dynamics of Job Segregation by Sex during World War II* (Urbana-Champaign: University of Illinois Press, 1987).

8. Litoff and Smith, *American Women in a World at War*, 167–68.

9. Sherna Berger Gluck, *Rosie the Riveter Revisited: Women, the War, and Social Change* (New York: Plume, 1987), 261.

10. Betty Friedan, *The Feminine Mystique* (New York: Norton, 1963), 58.

11. Lynn White Jr., *Educating Our Daughters* (New York: Harper and Brothers, 1950), 18.

12. *Ibid.*

13. Claudia Goldin, "The Role of World War II in the Rise of Women's Employment," *American Economic Review* 81, no. 4 (September 1991): 741–56.

14. Jeneane Lesko, "League History," Official Website of the AAGPBL: All-American Girls Professional Baseball League Players Association, accessed November 9, 2015, http://aagpbl.org/index.cfm/pages/league/12/league-history.

15. Male professional baseball players, many of whom belonged to the newly formed American Baseball Guild, were paid a minimum salary of $5,000. Player salaries for the 1940s topped out at $100,000, earned by Joe DiMaggio in 1949. Michael Haupert, "MLB's Annual Salary Leaders, 1874–2012," Society for American Baseball Research, last updated March 30, 2013, accessed July 20, 2013, http://sabr.org/research/mlbs-annual-salary-leaders-1874–2012.

16. Maybelle Blair, interview by author, Palm Springs, California, January 24, 2008.

17. Isabel "Lefty" Alvarez, interview by author, Palm Springs, California, February 16, 2009.

18. Delores Brumfield White, interview by Frank Boring, Milwaukee, Wisconsin, September 27, 2009, Veterans History Project, Digital Collections, Special Collections and University Archives, Grand Valley State University Libraries, Allendale, Michigan, accessed November 9, 2015, http://cdm16015.contentdm.oclc.org/cdm/singleitem/collection/p15068coll11/id/52/rec/3.

19. Carol Pierman, "Baseball, Conduct, and True Womanhood," *Women's Studies Quarterly* 33, no. 1/2 (Spring 2005): 60–61.

20. Jane Moffet, interview by author, Cape May, New Jersey, May 9, 2006.

21. Maybelle Blair, interview by author.

22. At approximately 65 percent, the proportion of married American women was higher in 1950 than at any other time between 1911 and 2011. Julissa Cruz, "Marriage: More than a Century of Change," National Center for Family & Marriage Research, Bowling Green State University, accessed November 22, 2015, www.bgsu.edu/content/dam/BGSU/college-of-arts-and-sciences/NCFMR/documents/FP/FP-13–13.pdf; see also 1997 AAGPBL questionnaire, Questionnaire file, Collection "AAGPBL," National Baseball Hall of Fame Archives, Cooperstown, New York.

23. Terry Donahue, interview by author, via telephone, June 10, 2007.

24. All quotations in this section come from Frank Boring's interview of Delores Brumfield White.

25. Earlene "Beans" Risinger, interview by Frank Boring, n.d., Veterans History Project, Digital Collections, Special Collections and University Archives, Grand Valley State University Libraries, Allendale, Michigan, accessed November 9, 2015, http://cdm16015.contentdm.oclc.org/cdm/singleitem/collection/p15068coll11/id/16/rec/3.

26. Jim Sargent, "Risinger, Earlene 'Beans,'" Official Website of the AAGPBL: All-American Girls Professional Baseball League Players Association, accessed November 9, 2015, http://aagpbl.org/index.cfm/articles/risinger-earlene-beans/11.

27. *Ibid.*

28. Earlene "Beans" Risinger, interview by Frank Boring.

29. Sargent, "Risinger, Earlene 'Beans.'"

30. *Ibid.*

31. Earlene "Beans" Risinger, autobiography, https://www.aagpbl.org/index.cfm/profiles/risinger-earlene/123..

32. Isabel "Lefty" Alvarez, interview by author, Palm Springs, California, June 6, 2011.

33. *Ibid.*

34. *Ibid.*

35. Merrie Fidler, *The Origins and History of the All-American Girls Professional Baseball League* (Jefferson, NC: McFarland, 2006), 99 and 113.

36. Isabel "Lefty" Alvarez, interview by author, June 6, 2011.

37. Isabel "Lefty" Alvarez, interview by author, Palm Springs, California, June 11, 2011.

38. *Ibid.*

39. Isabel "Lefty" Alvarez, interview by author, Palm Springs, California, October 11, 2009.

40. *Ibid.*

41. *Ibid.*

42. *Ibid.*

43. *Ibid.*

44. *Ibid.*

45. Joyce Hill Westerman, interview by James Smither, August 7, 2010, Veterans History Project, Digital Collections, Special Collections and University Archives, Grand Valley State University Libraries, Allendale, Michigan, accessed November 9, 2015, http://cdm16015.contentdm.oclc.org/cdm/singleitem/collection/p15068coll11/id/52/rec/3.

Chapter 2

1. Margaret Mead, *Coming of Age in Samoa* (New York: William Morrow, 1928), 1.

2. Mary Moore, interview by James Smither, August 7, 2010, Veterans History Project, Digital Collections, Special Collections and University Archives, Grand Valley State University Libraries, Allendale, Michigan, accessed November 9, 2015, http://cdm16015.contentdm.oclc.org/cdm/singleitem/collection/p15068coll11/id/46/rec/2.

3. Merrie Fidler, *The Origins and History of the All-American Girls Professional Baseball League* (Jefferson, NC: McFarland, 2006), 95.

4. *Ibid.*, 103–4.

5. *Ibid.*, 98.

6. "History of the League during 1947 & 1948," box "Dailey Records, 1943–1946," Joyce Sports Research Collection, Special Collection, University of Notre Dame Library, South Bend, Indiana.

7. Fidler, *Origins and History*, 111.

8. *Ibid.*, 112–13.

9. Copy of South American tour schedule, August 15, 1947, folder "S. A. Tour," Drawer 74, Meyerhoff Files, Northern Indiana Center for History, South Bend, Indiana.

10. Mary Rountree to Max Carey, January 31, 1948, folder "S. A. Tour," Drawer 74, Meyerhoff Files, Northern Indiana Center for History, South Bend, Indiana.

11. Fidler, *Origins and History*, 115.

12. AAGPBL News Release, February

10, 1949, folder "Tour Publicity," Drawer 74, Meyerhoff Files, Northern Indiana Center for History, South Bend, Indiana.

13. Ruth Richard diary, entry dated October 10–12, 1949, as quoted in Fidler, *Origins and History*, 120.

14. All quotes in this section are from James Smither's interview of Norma Dearfield, August 7, 2010, Veterans History Project, Digital Collections, Special Collections and University Archives, Grand Valley State University Libraries, Allendale, Michigan, accessed November 9, 2015, http://cdm16015.contentdm. oclc.org/cdm/singleitem/collection/p15068coll11/id/31/rec/1.

15. Patricia Brown, *A League of My Own: Memoirs of a Pitcher for the All-American Girls Professional Baseball League* (Jefferson, NC: McFarland, 2003), 180–81.

16. This quote and all subsequent quotes in this section are taken from James Smither's interview of Mary Moore.

17. Ann Petrovic, interview by James Smither, August 7, 2010, Veterans History Project, Digital Collections, Special Collections and University Archives, Grand Valley State University Libraries, Allendale, Michigan, accessed November 9, 2015, http://cdm16015.contentdm. oclc.org/cdm/singleitem/collection/p15068coll11/id/29/rec/1.

18. *Ibid.*

19. Katie Horstman, as quoted in Fidler, *Origins and History*, 160–62.

20. *Ibid.*, 159.

21. *Brown v. Board of Education of Topeka*, 347 U.S. 483 (1954).

22. Katie Horstman, interview by author, Palm Springs, California, January 25, 2008.

23. *Ibid.*

24. Joyce Hill Westerman, interview by James Smither, August 7, 2010, Veterans History Project, Digital Collections, Special Collections and University Archives, Grand Valley State University Libraries, Allendale, Michigan, accessed November 9, 2015, http://cdm16015. contentdm.oclc.org/cdm/singleitem/collection/p15068coll11/id/52/rec/3.

25. Audrey Daniels, interview by Frank Boring, August 5, 2010, Veterans History Project, Digital Collections, Special Collections and University Archives, Grand Valley State University Libraries, Allendale, Michigan, accessed November 9, 2015, http://cdm16015.contentdm. oclc.org/cdm/singleitem/collection/p15068coll11/id/30/rec/1.

26. *Ibid.*

27. Isabel "Lefty" Alvarez, interview by author, Palm Springs, California, October 11, 2009.

28. Katie Horstman, interview by author, Palm Springs, California, January 25, 2008.

29. All quotes from Jane Moffet are taken from the author's interview with her in Cape May, New Jersey, May 9, 2006.

30. Both of these interactions were witnessed by the author in Kalamazoo, Michigan, on August 29, 2004.

31. Marie "Blackie" Wegman, as quoted in Fidler, *Origins and History*, 98.

32. Joyce Westerman, interview by James Smither.

33. *Ibid.*

34. *Ibid.*

35. *Ibid.*

36. Helen Campbell, interview by author, Palm Springs, California, January 22, 2008.

37. Terry Donahue, interview by James Smither, August 4, 2010, Veterans History Project, Digital Collections, Special Collections and University Archives, Grand Valley State University Libraries, Allendale, Michigan, accessed November 9, 2015, http://cdm16015.contentdm. oclc.org/cdm/singleitem/collection/p15068coll11/id/50/rec/2.

38. Helen Filarski Steffes, interview by Frank Boring, August 5, 2010, Veterans History Project, Digital Collections, Special Collections and University Archives, Grand Valley State University

Libraries, Allendale, Michigan, accessed November 9, 2015, http://cdm16015. contentdm.oclc.org/cdm/singleitem/ collection/p15068coll11/id/32/rec/1.

39. Isabel "Lefty" Alvarez, interview by author, October 11, 2009.

40. *Ibid.*

41. Sam Purdy, "Revolutionary Béisbol: Political Appropriations of 'America's Game' in Pre- and Post-Revolution Nicaragua," *Yale Historical Review* 1, no. 2 (Spring 2010): 7.

42. Tiby Eisen, as quoted in Fidler, *Origins and History*, 119.

43. Isabel "Lefty" Alvarez, interview by author, October 11, 2009.

44. Merrie Fidler, *The Origins and History of the All-American Girls Professional Baseball League* (Jefferson, NC: McFarland, 2006), 119

45. "Empatada ayer la Serie de Baseball Femenino," *La Nueva Prensa* (Managua, Nicaragua), 4 de Febrero de 1949, as quoted in Fidler, *Origins and History*, 120.

46. Isabel "Lefty" Alvarez, interview by author, October 11, 2009.

47. *Ibid.*

Chapter 3

1. Private John E. Stevenson, *The Sporting News* (April 1942): 5.

2. Earlene "Beans" Risinger, interview by Frank Boring, n.d., Veterans History Project, Digital Collections, Special Collections and University Archives, Grand Valley State University Libraries, Allendale, Michigan, accessed November 9, 2015, http://cdm16015.contentdm. oclc.org/cdm/singleitem/collection/ p15068coll11/id/16/rec/3.

3. *Ibid.*

4. Merrie Fidler, *The Origins and History of the All-American Girls Professional Baseball League* (Jefferson, NC: McFarland, 2006), 32–33.

5. Jeneane Lesko, "League History," Official Website of the AAGPBL: All-

American Girls Professional Baseball League Players Association, accessed November 9, 2015, http://aagpbl.org/index. cfm/pages/league/12/league-history.

6. Jacqueline Baumgart, interview by Frank Boring, n.d., Veterans History Project, Digital Collections, Special Collections and University Archives, Grand Valley State University Libraries, Allendale, Michigan, accessed November 9, 2015, http://cdm16015.contentdm.oclc. org/cdm/singleitem/collection/p15068 coll11/id/23/rec/1.

7. Joyce McCoy, interview by Gordon Olson, September 27, 2009, Veterans History Project, Digital Collections, Special Collections and University Archives, Grand Valley State University Libraries, Allendale, Michigan, accessed November 9, 2015, http://cdm16015. contentdm.oclc.org/cdm/singleitem/ collection/p15068coll11/id/42/rec/2.

8. Fidler, *Origins and History*, 51.

9. Advertisement for the Kenosha Comets, *Kenosha Evening News*, June 1943, 9.

10. Joyce McCoy, interview by Gordon Olson.

11. Earlene "Beans" Risinger, interview by Frank Boring.

12. Karen Kunkel, interview by author, Syracuse, New York, September 12, 2003.

13. Jacqueline Baumgart, interview by Frank Boring.

14. All quotes from Jerre Denoble are taken from her interview with James Smither, August 8, 2010, Veterans History Project, Digital Collections, Special Collections and University Archives, Grand Valley State University Libraries, Allendale, Michigan, accessed November 9, 2015, http://cdm16015.contentdm. oclc.org/cdm/singleitem/collection/ p15068coll11/id/43/rec/1.

15. Mattie E. Treadwell, *The Women's Army Corps*, United States Army in World War II, Special Studies (1954; repr., Washington, DC: United States Army Center of Military History, 1991), 28–39.

16. More than 25,000 women applied to serve in the WASPs, but fewer than 1,900 were accepted. Virginia M. Hope, "History of the WASPS," Folder 1, "1942–44," Virginia Hope Papers, Minnesota Historical Society Library, St. Paul.

17. "Women and the U.S. Coast Guard: Moments in History," United States Coast Guard/U.S. Department of Homeland Security, accessed July 1, 2013, uscg.mil/history/uscghist/Women Chronology.asp.

18. Merrie Fidler, "Baseball's Women on the Field During WWII," in *Who's on First: Replacement Players in World War II*, edited by Marc Z. Aaron and Bill Nowlin, with associate editors James Forr and Len Levin (Phoenix, AZ: SABR, 2015), 374–89.

19. All quotes in this section are taken from Helen "Gig" Smith, interview, n.d., Veterans History Project, Digital Collections, Special Collections and University Archives, Grand Valley State University Libraries, Allendale, Michigan, accessed November 9, 2015, http://cdm16015.contentdm.oclc.org/cdm/singleitem/collection/p15068coll11/id/8/rec/3.

20. Cpl. Deanna McDaniel, "Helen Hannah Campbell, U.S. Marine," Official Website of the AAGPBL, accessed August 14, 2012, http://aagpbl.org/index.cfm/profiles/campbell-helen-hannah/703.

21. *Ibid.*

22. *Ibid.*

23. Patricia Brown, *A League of My Own: Memoirs of a Pitcher for the All-American Girls Professional Baseball League* (Jefferson, NC: McFarland, 2003), 157.

24. McDaniel, "Helen Hannah Campbell."

25. Helen Campbell, interview by author, Palm Springs, California, January 22, 2008.

26. All quotes from Elma "Steck" Weiss are taken from her interview with James Smither, August 7, 2010, Veterans History Project, Digital Collections, Special Collections and University Archives, Grand Valley State University Libraries, Allendale, Michigan, accessed November 9, 2015. contentdm.oclc.org/cdm/singleitem/collection/p15068coll11/id/28/rec/1.

Chapter 4

1. Isabel "Lefty" Alvarez, interview by author, via telephone, October 20, 2011.

2. U.S. Government Accountability Office, "Intercollegiate Athletics: Four-Year Colleges' Experiences Adding and Discontinuing Teams," March 2001, GAO-01–297, U.S. Government Accountability Office, accessed November 22, 2015, http://gao.gov/products/GAO-01–297.

3. "High School Participation Increases for 25th Consecutive Year," last modified October 2014, National Federation of State High School Associations (NFHS), accessed November 30, 2015, http://nfhs.org/articles/high-school-participation-increases-for-25th-consecutive-year.

4. OppenheimerFunds, "New Nationwide Research Finds: Successful Women Business Executives Don't Just Talk a Good Game … They Play(ed) One," PR Newswire, last updated February 8, 2002, accessed July 19, 2015, www.prnewswire.com/news-releases/new-nationwide-research-finds-successful-women-business-executives-dont-just-talk-a-good-game-they-played-one-75898622.html.

5. *Empowering Women in Sports*, The Empowering Women Series, no. 4 (Arlington, VA: Feminist Majority Foundation, 1995), accessed December 15, 2015, http://feminist.org/research/sports/sports2.html.

6. *Ibid.*

7. Audrey Daniels, interview by Frank Boring, August 5, 2010, Veterans History Project, Digital Collections, Special

Collections and University Archives, Grand Valley State University Libraries, Allendale, Michigan, accessed November 9, 2015, http://cdm16015.contentdm. oclc.org/cdm/singleitem/collection/ p15068coll11/id/30/rec/1.

8. The breadth of the players' continued involvement in sports can be seen in the surveys conducted by the National Baseball Hall of Fame. See 1997 AAGPBL questionnaire, Questionnaire file, Collection "AAGPBL," National Baseball Hall of Fame Archives, Cooperstown, New York.

9. Earlene "Beans" Risinger, interview by Frank Boring, n.d., Veterans History Project, Digital Collections, Special Collections and University Archives, Grand Valley State University Libraries, Allendale, Michigan, accessed November 9, 2015, http://cdm16015.contentdm. oclc.org/cdm/singleitem/collection/ p15068coll11/id/16/rec/3.

10. *Ibid.*

11. Mary Pratt, interview by Frank Boring, September 27, 2009, Veterans History Project, Digital Collections, Special Collections and University Archives, Grand Valley State University Libraries, Allendale, Michigan, accessed November 9, 2015, http://cdm16015.contentdm. oclc.org/cdm/singleitem/collection/ p15068coll11/id/9/rec/4.

12. Earlene "Beans" Risinger, interview by Frank Boring.

13. Terry Donahue, interview by author, via telephone, September 14, 2008.

14. Baseball-Reference.com, "Wagner, Audrey (12/27/1927–8/31/1984)," Official Website of the AAGPBL: All-American Girls Professional Baseball League Players Association, accessed November 9, 2015, http://aagpbl.org/ index.cfm/articles/wagner-audrey-12– 27-1927—8-31-1984/291.

15. National Baseball Hall of Fame questionnaire filled out by Audrey Wagner's brother after her death; see 1997 AAGPBL questionnaire, National Baseball Hall of Fame.

16. Patricia Brown, *A League of My Own: Memoirs of a Pitcher for the All-American Girls Professional Baseball League* (Jefferson, NC: McFarland, 2003), 164–65.

17. *Ibid.*, 166.

18. *Ibid.*, 165–66.

19. *Ibid.*, 169.

20. *Ibid.*, 168.

21. Katie Horstman, interview by author, Palm Springs, California, January 25, 2008.

22. "Class of 1986," Hall of Fame, Ohio Association of Track and Cross Country Coaches, accessed November 22, 2015, http://oatccc.com/halloffame/ 1986.html.

23. Bob Huelsman, "In a League of Her Own ... Katie Horstman," *Press Pros Magazine*, May 11, 2011, http://presspros magazine.com/in-a-league-of-her-own-katie-horstman.

24. "Jean Cione," Official Website of the AAGPBL: All-American Girls Professional Baseball League Players Association, accessed November 9, 2015, http://aagpbl.org/index.cfm/profiles/ cione-jean/221.

25. *Ibid.*

26. *Ibid.*

27. Charles Faber, "Kunkel, Karen Violetta," Official Website of the AAGPBL: All-American Girls Professional Baseball League Players Association, accessed November 9, 2015, http://aagpbl. org/index.cfm/articles/kunkel-karen-violetta/174.

28. Jeneane Lesko, interview by James Smither, August 4, 2010, Veterans History Project, Digital Collections, Special Collections and University Archives, Grand Valley State University Libraries, Allendale, Michigan, accessed November 9, 2015, http://cdm16015.contentdm. oclc.org/cdm/singleitem/collection/ p15068coll11/id/40/rec/1.

29. Betsy Jochum, interview by James Smither, August 4, 2010, Veterans History Project, Digital Collections, Special Collections and University Archives,

Grand Valley State University Libraries, Allendale, Michigan, accessed November 9, 2015, http://cdm16015.contentdm. oclc.org/cdm/singleitem/collection/ p15068coll11/id/33/rec/2.

Chapter 5

1. Terry Donahue, interview by author, via telephone, September 14, 2008.
2. Isabel "Lefty" Alvarez, interview by author, via telephone, October 20, 2011.
3. Shirley Burkovich, interview by James Smither, n.d., Veterans History Project, Digital Collections, Special Collections and University Archives, Grand Valley State University Libraries, Allendale, Michigan, accessed November 9, 2015, http://cdm16015.contentdm.oclc. org/cdm/singleitem/collection/ p15068coll11/id/26/rec/1.
4. Isabel "Lefty" Alvarez, interview by author, October 20, 2011.
5. Ed Des Lauriers, as quoted in Merrie Fidler, *The Origins and History of the All-American Girls Professional Baseball League* (Jefferson, NC: McFarland, 2006), 229.
6. Fidler, *Origins and History*, 229–30.
7. One of the first academic explorations was Merrie Fidler's "The Development and Decline of the All-American Girls Professional Baseball League, 1943–1954," master's thesis, University of Massachusetts, Amherst, 1976.
8. Fidler, *Origins and History*, 231.
9. *Ibid.*, 231–32.
10. June Peppas, as quoted in Fidler, *Origins and History*, 232.
11. *Ibid.*, 234.
12. Fidler, *Origins and History*, 235–36.
13. Ruth Davis, as quoted in Fidler, *Origins and History*, 236.
14. AAGPBL advertisement, as quoted in Fidler, *Origins and History*, 237.
15. Audrey Daniels, interview by

Frank Boring, August 5, 2010, Veterans History Project, Digital Collections, Special Collections and University Archives, Grand Valley State University Libraries, Allendale, Michigan, accessed November 9, 2015, http://cdm16015.contentdm. oclc.org/cdm/singleitem/collection/ p15068coll11/id/30/rec/1.
16. Isabell "Lefty" Alvarez, interview by author, Palm Springs, California, October 11, 2009.
17. *Ibid.*
18. *Ibid.*
19. *Ibid.*
20. *Ibid.*
21. Kelly Candaele, as quoted in Fidler, *Origins and History*, 279.
22. From the AAGPBL newsletter *Extra Innings* (April 1986), n.p., author's personal collection.
23. Fidler, *Origins and History*, 251.
24. *Ibid.*, 258–59.
25. Ted Spencer, as quoted in Fidler, *Origins and History*, 259.
26. Penny Marshall, foreword to Jane Gottesman's *Game Face: What Does a Female Athlete Look Like?* (New York: Random House, 2001), 9.
27. *Ibid.*
28. *A League of Their Own*, directed by Penny Marshall, Parkway Productions, July 1992.
29. Shirley Burkovich, interview by author, Palm Springs, California, January 23, 2008.
30. Terry Donahue, interview by James Smither, August 4, 2010, Veterans History Project, Digital Collections, Special Collections and University Archives, Grand Valley State University Libraries, Allendale, Michigan, accessed November 9, 2015, http://cdm16015.contentdm. oclc.org/cdm/singleitem/collection/ p15068coll11/id/50/rec/2.
31. Patricia Brown, *A League of My Own: Memoirs of a Pitcher for the All-American Girls Professional Baseball League* (Jefferson, NC: McFarland, 2003), 121.
32. Maybelle Blair, interview by James

Smither, September 27, 2009, Veterans History Project, Digital Collections, Special Collections and University Archives, Grand Valley State University Libraries, Allendale, Michigan, accessed November 9, 2015, http://cdm16015.contentdm. oclc.org/cdm/singleitem/collection/ p15068coll11/id/15/rec/1.

33. Terry Donahue, interview by James Smither.

34. Wilma Briggs, as quoted in Fidler, *Origins and History*, 286.

35. Fidler, *Origins and History*, 287.

36. Earlene "Beans" Risinger, interview by Frank Boring, n.d., Veterans History Project, Digital Collections, Special Collections and University Archives, Grand Valley State University Libraries, Allendale, Michigan, accessed November 9, 2015, http://cdm16015.contentdm. oclc.org/cdm/singleitem/collection/ p15068coll11/id/16/rec/3.

37. Shirley Burkovich, interview by author, January 23, 2008.

38. Joyce M. Smith, "Risinger, Earlene 'Beans,'" Official Website of the AAGPBL: All-American Girls Professional Baseball League Players Association, accessed November 9, 2015, http://aagpbl.org/ index.cfm/articles/risinger-earlene-beans/18.

39. Shirley Burkovich, interview by author, Orlando, Florida, June 3, 2015.

40. Kristen Huff, unpublished manuscript, author's personal collection.

Chapter 6

1. Maybelle Blair, interview by author, Orlando, Florida, June 1, 2015.

2. *Ibid.*

3. Terry Donahue, interview by author, via telephone, September 14, 2008.

4. Jeneane Lesko, "League History," Official Website of the AAGPBL: All-American Girls Professional Baseball League Players Association, accessed November 9, 2015, http://aagpbl.org/index. cfm/pages/league/12/league-history.

5. Merrie Fidler, *The Origins and History of the All-American Girls Professional Baseball League* (Jefferson, NC: McFarland, 2006), 161.

6. Katie Horstman, interview by author, Palm Springs, California, July 17, 2011.

7. Fidler, *Origins and History*, 161.

8. Lefty Alvarez, telephone interview by author, October 20, 2011.

9. Jean Ardell, *Breaking into Baseball: Women and the National Pastime* (Carbondale: Southern Illinois Press, 2005), 144–45.

10. Maybelle Blair, interview by author, Palm Springs, California, July 23, 2011.

11. Pawtucket Slaterettes Baseball League, accessed April 14, 2016, http:// womeninbaseball.com/press-media-coverage/slaterettes-in-own-league.

12. Ardell, *Breaking into Baseball*, 85–86.

13. Maybelle Blair, interview by author, July 23, 2011.

14. Little League Baseball, accessed April 15, 2016, www.littleleague.org/ media/llnewsarchive/06_2003/03_30th girls.htm.

15. Ardell, *Breaking into Baseball*, 97–98.

16. Little League Baseball.

17. Ardell, *Breaking into Baseball*, 121.

18. Colorado Silver Bullets, accessed April 10, 2016, www.coloradosilver bullets.org.

19. *Ibid.*

20. Ardell, *Breaking into Baseball*, 121–22.

21. *Ibid.*, 122.

22. Maybelle Blair, interview by author, Orlando, Florida, June 2, 2015.

23. *Ibid.*

24. Ardell, *Breaking into Baseball*, 97–98.

25. Women's Baseball History, USA Baseball, accessed April 19, 2016, http:// web.usabaseball.com/playball/womens-baseball/history.

26. Resources, AAU Sports, accessed April 15, 2016, http://ww3.aausports.org/Resources/AboutAAU.aspx.
27. Maybelle Blair, interview by author, Orlando, Florida, June 2, 2015.
28. Shirley Burkovich, interview by author, Orlando, Florida, June 3, 2015.
29. Grace DeVinney, email exchange, April 17, 2016.
30. Karen and Josh DeVinney, email exchange, April 17, 2016.
31. *Ibid.*
32. Emma Charlesworth-Seiler, "Stealing Home: Why Baseball Isn't America's National Pastime," master's thesis, Department of Sociology, Hamline University, 2016.
33. Matthew Muench, "More Girls Playing High School Baseball," *ESPN High School* (blog), October 17, 2011, accessed April 20, 2016, http://espn.go.com/blog/high-school/baseball/post/_/id/519/changing-the-game-girls-in-high-school-baseball.
34. Women's Baseball History, USA Baseball.
35. Maybelle Blair, interview by author, June 2, 2015.
36. *Ibid.*

Conclusion

1. Ron was my cousin, and it was on his deathbed that we had this conversation about my future as a college professor. Ron Webb, conversation with author, Leitchfield, Kentucky, June 1994.
2. Delores Brumfield White, interview by Frank Boring, September 27, 2009, Veterans History Project, Digital Collections, Special Collections and University Archives, Grand Valley State University Libraries, Allendale, Michigan, accessed November 9, 2015, http://cdm16015.contentdm.oclc.org/cdm/singleitem/collection/p15068coll11/id/24/rec/1.
3. Janet "Pee Wee" Wiley, as quoted in Patricia Brown, *A League of My Own: Memoirs of a Pitcher for the All-American Girls Professional Baseball League* (Jefferson, NC: McFarland, 2003), 167.
4. I introduce this concept in Kat D. Williams, "Sport: 'A Useful Category of Historical Analysis': Isabel 'Lefty' Alvarez: The Rascal of El Cerro," *International Journal of the History of Sport* 29, no. 5 (Special Issue: Sport, Women, Society: International Perspectives, 2012): 766–85.
5. Maddy English, quoted in Brown, *A League of My Own*, 167.
6. Jacqueline "Jackie" Mattson, quoted in Brown, *A League of My Own*, 174.
7. Isabel "Lefty" Alvarez, interview by author, Palm Springs, California, June 6, 2011.
8. Maybelle Blair, interview by author, Palm Springs, California, July 23, 2011.
9. Isabel "Lefty" Alvarez, interview by author, June 6, 2011.

Bibliography

Ardell, Jean. *Breaking into Baseball: Women and the National Pastime*. Carbondale: Southern Illinois Press, 2005.

Berlage, Gai. *Women in Baseball: The Forgotten History*. Westport, CT: Praeger, 1994.

Brown, Patricia. *A League of My Own: Memoirs of a Pitcher for the All-American Girls Professional Baseball League*. Jefferson, NC: McFarland, 2003.

Browne, Lois. *The Girls of Summer: The Real Story of the All-American Girls Professional Baseball League*. New York: HarperCollins, 1992.

Bullock, Steven R. *Playing for Their Nation: Baseball and the American Military during World War II*. Lincoln: University of Nebraska Press, 2004.

Cahn, Susan. *Coming on Strong: Gender and Sexuality in Twentieth-Century Women's Sport*. Cambridge, MA: Harvard University Press, 1998.

Chang, R.S., and J.M. Culp. "After Intersectionality." *University of Missouri–Kansas City Law Review* 71 (2002): 485–91.

Crenshaw, Kimberle Williams. "Mapping the Margins: Intersectionality, Identity Politics, and Violence against Women of Color." In *Public Nature of Private Violence*, edited by Martha Albertson Fineman and Roxanne Mykitiuk, 93–118. New York: Routledge, 1994.

Cruz, Julissa. "Marriage: More than a Century of Change." National Center for Family & Marriage Research, Bowling Green State University. Accessed November 22, 2015. www.bgsu.edu/content/dam/BGSU/college-of-arts-and-sciences/NCFMR/documents/FP/FP-13–13.pdf.

Empowering Women in Sports. The Empowering Women Series, no. 4. Arlington, VA: Feminist Majority Foundation, 1995. Accessed December 15, 2015. http://feminist.org/research/sports/sports2.html.

Fidler, Merrie. "Baseball's Women on the Field during WWII." In *Who's on First: Replacement Players in World War II*, edited by Marc Z. Aaron and Bill Nowlin, with associate editors James Forr and Len Levin, 374–89. Phoenix, AZ: SABR, 2015.

_____. *The Origins and History of the All-American Girls Professional Baseball League*. Jefferson, NC: McFarland, 2006.

Fincher, Jack. "The 'Belles of the Game' Were a Hit with Their Fans." *Smithsonian* 20 (1999): 88–97.

Friedan, Betty. *The Feminine Mystique*. New York: Norton, 1963.

169

Bibliography

Galt, Margot Fortunato. *Up to the Plate: The All American Girls Professional Baseball League.* Minneapolis: Lerner, 1995.

Gilbert, Sarah. *A League of Their Own* (novelization). New York: Warner, 1992.

Gluck, Sherna Berger. *Rosie the Riveter Revisited: Women, the War, and Social Change.* New York: Plume, 1987.

Goldin, Claudia. "The Role of World War II in the Rise of Women's Employment." *American Economic Review* 81, no. 4 (September 1991): 741–56.

Gottsman, Jane. *Game Face: What Does a Female Athlete Look Like?* New York: Random House, 2001.

Gregorich, Barbara. *Women at Play: The Story of Women in Baseball.* San Diego: Harcourt Brace, 1993.

Hanmer, Trudy J. *The All-American Girls Professional Baseball League. American Events Series.* New York: New Discovery, 1994.

Hartmann-Tews, Ilse, and Gertrud Pfister. *Sport and Women: Social Issues in International Perspective.* New York: Routledge, 2005.

Helmer, Diana Star. *Belles of the Ballpark.* Brookfield, CT: Millbrook, 1993.

Howe, Louise Kapp. *Pink Collar Workers: Inside the World of Women's Work.* New York: G.P Putnam and Sons, 1977.

Huelsman, Bob. "In a League of Her Own ... Katie Horstman." *Press Pros Magazine,* May 11, 2011. http://pressprosmagazine.com/in-a-league-of-her-own-katie-horstman.

Huff, Kristen. Unpublished manuscript, October 2013. Author's collection.

Johnson, Susan E. *When Women Played Hardball.* Seattle: Seal, 1994.

Kovach, John. *Benders: Tales from South Bend's Baseball Past.* South Bend, IN: Greenstocking, 1987.

Litoff, Judy Barrett, and David Smith. *American Women in a World at War: Contemporary Accounts from World War II.* The Worlds of Women Series. Lanham, MD: Rowman & Littlefield, 1997.

Madden, W.C. *The All-American Girls Professional Baseball League Record Book: Comprehensive Hitting, Fielding and Pitching Statistics.* Jefferson, NC: McFarland, 2000.

_____. *The Hoosiers of Summer.* Indianapolis, IN: Guild, 1994.

_____. *The Women of the All-American Girls Professional Baseball League: A Biographical Dictionary.* Jefferson, NC: McFarland, 1997.

Mead, Margaret. *Coming of Age in Samoa.* New York: William Morrow, 1928.

Milkman, Ruth. *Gender at Work: The Dynamics of Job Segregation by Sex during World War II.* Urbana-Champaign: University of Illinois Press, 1987.

Miller, Ernestine. *Making Her Mark: Firsts and Milestones in Women's Sports.* New York: McGraw-Hill, 2002.

Muench, Matthew. "More Girls Playing High School Baseball." *ESPN High School* (blog), October 17, 2011. http://espn.go.com/blog/high-school/baseball/post/_/id/519/changing-the-game-girls-in-high-school-baseball.

OppenheimerFunds. "New Nationwide Research Finds: Successful Women Business Executives Don't Just Talk a Good Game ... They Play(ed) One." PR Newswire, last updated February 8, 2002. Accessed July 19, 2015. www.prnewswire.com/news-releases/new-nationwide-research-finds-successful-women-business-executives-dont-just-talk-a-good-game-they-played-one-75898622.html.

Osborne, Carol A., and Fiona Skillen. *Women in Sports History*. New York: Routledge, 2012.

Park, Roberta J., and Patricia Vertinsky. *Women, Sport, Society: Further Reflections, Reaffirming Mary Wollstonecraft*. New York: Routledge, 2011.

Pidgeon, Mary. *Changes in Women's Employment during the War*. Washington, DC: U.S. Department of Labor, Women's Bureau, 1944.

_____. *Women's Work and the War*. American Job Series Occupational Monograph No. 36. Chicago: Science Research Association, 1943.

Pierman, Carol J. *"The All-American Girls Professional Baseball League: Accomplishing Great Things in a Dangerous World."* In *Across the Diamond: Essays on Baseball and American Culture*, edited by Edward J. Rielly, 97–108. Binghamton, NY: Haworth, 2003.

_____. "Baseball, Conduct, and True Womanhood." *Women's Studies Quarterly* 33, no. 1/2 (Spring 2005): 60–85.

Pratt, Mary. *A Peach of a Game*. Quincy, MA: Self-published, 2004.

Purdy, Sam. "Revolutionary Béisbol: Political Appropriations of 'America's Game' in Pre- and Post-Revolution Nicaragua." *Yale Historical Review* 1, no. 2 (Spring 2010): 6–18.

Ring, Jennifer. *A Game of Their Own: Voice of Contemporary Women in Baseball*. Lincoln: University of Nebraska Press, 2015.

Roepke, Sharon. *Diamond Gals*. Kalamazoo, MI: Self-published, 1986.

Scott, Joan. "Gender: A Useful Category of Historical Analysis." *American Historical Review* 91, no. 5 (1986): 1053–75.

Seymour Mills, Dorothy, and Harold Seymour. *Baseball: The People's Game*. New York: Oxford University Press, 1990.

Smith, Lissa, ed. *Nike Is a Goddess: The History of Women in Sports*. New York: Atlantic Monthly, 1999.

Stevenson, Private John E. *The Sporting News* (April 1942).

Stevenson, Rosemary, and W.C. Madden. *Don't Die on Third*. Monticello, NY: Madden, 2006.

Treadwell, Mattie E. *The Women's Army Corps*. United States Army in World War II, Special Studies. 1954; reprint, Washington, DC: United States Army Center of Military History, 1991.

Trombe, Carolyn. *Dottie Wiltse Collins: Strikeout Queen of the All-American Girls Professional Baseball League*. Jefferson, NC: McFarland, 2005.

Ware, Susan. "Women and the Great Depression." Gilder Lehrman Institute of American History. Accessed on November 9, 2015. www.gilderlehrman.org/history-by-era/great-depression/essays/women-and-great-depression.

White, Lynn, Jr. *Educating Our Daughters*. New York: Harper and Brothers, 1950.

Woolf, Virginia. *A Room of One's Own*. New York: Harcourt, Brace, 1929.

Yellin, Emily. *Our Mothers' War: American Women at Home and at the Front during World War II*. 2004; reprint, New York: Free, 2005.

Dissertations and Theses

Charlesworth-Seiler, Emma. "Stealing Home: Why Baseball Isn't America's National Pastime." Master's thesis, Department of Sociology, Hamline University, 2016.

Bibliography

Fidler, Merrie. *"The Development and Decline of the All-American Girls Professional Baseball League, 1943–1954."* Master's thesis, University of Massachusetts, Amherst, 1976.

Hensley, Beth H. *"Older Women's Life Choices and Development after Playing Professional Baseball."* EdD dissertation, University of Cincinnati, 1995.

Sexton, Maria. *"Implications of the All-American Girls Baseball League for Physical Educators in the Guidance of Highly-Skilled Girls."* Type C Project, Advanced School of Education, Teachers College, Columbia University, 1953.

Shattuck, Debbie. *"Playing a Man's Game: Women in Baseball in the U.S."* Master's thesis, University of Colorado, Colorado Springs, 1993.

Archives, Collections and Websites

AAU Sports website. http://ww3.aausports.org.

All-American Girls Professional Baseball League Collection. National Baseball Hall of Fame Archives, Cooperstown, New York.

Colorado Silver Bullets. Colorado Springs, Colorado. www.coloradosilverbullets.org.

Little League Baseball. www.littleleague.org.

Minnesota Historical Society Library, St. Paul.

National Federation of State High School Associations. http://nfhs.org.

Northern Indiana Center for History, South Bend, Indiana.

Official Website of the AAGPBL: All-American Girls Professional Baseball League Players Association. http://aagpbl.org.

Ohio Association of Track and Cross Country Coaches. http://oatccc.com.

Society for American Baseball Research. http://sabr.org.

Tucker Institute for Research on Girls and Women in Sport, University of Minnesota. www.cehd.umn.edu/tuckercenter/default.html.

U.S. Government Accountability Office. http://gao.gov.

USA Baseball. http://web.usabaseball.com.

Veterans History Project. Digital Collections, Special Collections and University Archives, Grand Valley State University Libraries, Allendale, Michigan. http://cdm16015.contentdm.oclc.org/cdm/singleitem/collection/p15068coll11.

Women's Sports Foundation. www.womenssportsfoundation.org.

Author-Conducted Oral Histories

Alvarez, Isabel "Lefty." Grand Rapids, Michigan, June 8, 2007; Palm Springs, California, February 16 and October 11, 2009, and June 6 and 11, 2011; telephone conversation, October 20, 2011.

Blair, Maybelle. Palm Springs, California, January 24, 2008, and July 23, 2011; Orlando, Florida, June 2 and 3, 2015.

Burkovich, Shirley. Palm Springs, California, January 23, 2008; Orlando, Florida, June 2 and 3, 2015.

Campbell, Helen. Palm Springs, California, January 22, 2008.

Bibliography

DeVinney, Grace. Email exchange, April 17, 2016.
DeVinney, Josh, and Karen DeVinney. Email exchange, April 17, 2016.
Donahue, Terry. Telephone interview, June 10, 2007, and September 14, 2008.
Horstman, Katie. Palm Springs, California, January 25, 2008, and July 17, 2011.
Kunkel, Karen. Syracuse, New York, September 12, 2003.
Lee, Annabelle. Palm Springs, California, September 19, 2006.
Moffet, Jane. Cape May, New Jersey, May 9, 2006.
Petrovic, Ann. Detroit, Michigan, August 7, 2010.
Westerman, Joyce. Detroit, Michigan, August 9, 2010.

Index

Numbers in *bold italics* indicate pages with photographs.

Index

Index

Index

Index